This piece of work is dedicated

to

My Family

and to All who have a

Passion for Knowledge

Introduction

Welcome Inquisitive Minds!

Knowledge is one prized possession which can be learnt and acquired, but cannot be bought or stolen. The quest and absorption of knowledge has made us humans, the most intelligent species despite having low brain mass.

It has been proven that short tid-bits of informatics are more effective in retention and recall than lengthy literary works. Since we all have interests in various fields, it is my attempt to shed some interesting snippets of information on diverse subjects.

Never Stop Learning!

KARL M

Table of Contents

Contents

Trivia Tid-bits

Panorama": is derived from Greek word 'pan' (meaning 'all') and 'horama' (meaning 'spectacle') The word 'panorama' was to describe an invention by the artist Robert Barker, an apparatus for showing pictures inside of a cylindrical surface, enabling the viewer to access 360-degree view.

"Origami": is a traditional Japanese art form of paper folding. The word is derived from the Japanese word "ori" (folding) and "kami" (paper). The best known example of 'origami' is "orizuru" (paper crane).

"Truffle" is a highly prized fungi called the "diamond of the kitchen'. Specially trained dogs & pigs are used to sniff out truffles. A chemical compound similar to adrostenol which is a sex pheromone found in the saliva of male pigs is found within the truffle which attracts female sows.

"Thunder and Lightning" is a common phrase. But in fact the "lightning" precedes "thunder" because light travels faster than sound. So the lightning is seen first followed by thunder.

"Emeritus" comes from the Latin verb "emerere" which translated means completion of service, and originally referred to a veteran soldier serving his time. Nowadays, it relates to professionals especially from Academics. The females are "Emerita" and the plural is "Emiriti"

Weather and Climate are at times used interchangeably. However, "weather" is a set of atmospheric conditions in one particular location for a short period of time like throughout the day, whereas "climate" is a set of conditions over a longer period probably in years.

"Choler" means anger, irritability, or bad temperament. In the medieval science of medicine 'choler' was one of the four basic humors whereby diseases were caused by these four substances getting out of sync or balance:

- Black bile (melancholia)
- Yellow bile (cholera)
- Phlegm (phlegma)
- Blood (sanguis)

The top 5 most common words used in English are, in the following order:

1. The
2. Be
3. To
4. Of
5. And

The most used words in English starts with the alphabet "S" and the least starts with the alphabet "X".

In Academics, "Ivy League" is used to define elite institutions of education in the USA. The 8 Ivy League Schools are: Brown, Columbia, Cornell, Dartmouth, Harvard, Princeton, Pennsylvania and Yale Universities.

Tattoo (or "tat" or "ink") derives from Tahitian word "tatau" which was used by the explorer Captain Cook when he described the indelible markings on the skin of Polynesian locals.

In the field of texting, new forms of numerical acronyms are gaining popularity such as:

- 2G2BT : Too Good To Be True
- 4COL: For Crying Out Loud.
- 404:   I Don't Know
- 459:   I Love You (ILY is 459 on keypad)
- 6Y: Sexy

Nicholas II ("Saint Nicholas the Passion-Bearer") was the last Emperor of Russia. He and his entire family were executed in the basement of their house by Bolsheviks led by Yakov Yurovsky. Mystery surrounded the survival of his youngest daughter Anastasia, with numerous women claiming to be her, until DNA analysis confirmed her execution in the basement.

"Nobel Prize" is named after the Swedish chemist Alfred Nobel, the inventor of Dynamite. There are a total of 5 awards every year in Physics, Chemistry, Physiology or Medicine, and Literature awarded in Sweden and the most important Peace Prize is awarded in Norway by the Norwegian Nobel Committee.

An Academic Degree is awarded to students upon completion of specific examinations of higher education. The three honours are denoted by specific Latin names, viz:

- cum-laude : meaning "with honour"
- magna cum-laude : meaning "with great honour"
- summa cum-laude : meaning "with greatest honour"

"Hydrogen Bomb" (H-Bomb) was first successfully tested by USA on atoll "Enewetak" in the Pacific Ocean, and was codenamed "Ivy Mike". The explosion achieved a yield 500 times larger than the Nagasaki bomb and made a crater 164 feet deep.

"Beryl" is a mineral compound with well-known varieties which includes Emerald and Aquamarine. Pure beryl is colourless, and is frequently tinted with impurities to give colours like green, blue, yellow, pink and red (rarest).

"Cameo Role" is a brief appearance in performing arts by well-known persons or celebrities. These appearances are generally for a very short duration and often a non-speaking role. Most notable among them are cameo roles by director Alfred Hitchcock in most of his movies.

Many people suffer from "Aerophobia" which is fear and anxiety of flying. To address this issue San Francisco International Airport has deployed a "wag brigade", a team of specially trained dogs to calm the nervous fliers. The canines wear vests which read "Pet Me".

The sensation caused by light tickling is known as "Knismesis" whereas the laughter caused by hard tickling is known as "Gargalesis". Apart from primates, the only other species to experience tickling are rats, though the females find the sensation adverse.

The closest the world came to a Nuclear War was during the 13 day stand-off between USA & USSR in 1962 known as the Cuban Missile Crisis. It triggered off by USSR deploying ballistic missiles in Cuba in response to US deployment of missiles in Turkey & Italy.

"Stockholm Syndrome" is a sympathetic psychological bond the hostages feel towards their captors. The term was coined when 4 hostages were taken during a bank robbery in Stockholm. The hostages refused to testify against their captors; in fact they even defended their actions.

"Numismatics" is the study of coins and paper money. The "obverse" side of a coin is referred to as "heads" as it depicts the head of a prominent personality and the "reverse" is known as "tails" as it is the opposite of heads.

Oval Office" (being "oval" shaped) is the formal working space of "POTUS" (President of the United States) which has four doors: the East door opens to Rose Garden, West door opens to private study & Dining room, Northwest opens to the main corridor & Northeast opens to the office of the President's Secretary.

Alcoholics Anonymous ("AA") is an international abstinence based recovery program from alcoholism founded by Bill Wilson & Bob Smith in USA. It is a 12 step based program with initially admitting to powerlessness over the use of alcohol.

"Toque" is a traditional white brimless hat worn by chefs in the kitchen. Generally the hat consists of 100 'pleats' (folds) which signifies the number of types an egg can be prepared. The difference in heights of the toque also signifies the rank of the chef in the kitchen.

Most homes world-wide are supplied with natural gas which is naturally odourless. In order to detect a leak, a tiny amount of tert-Butylthiol is added which is a organosulphur compound. In the event of a leak it emits an smell like rotten eggs.

"Honeymoon" originally meant married couples taking a "bridal tour" to visit relatives who could not attend their wedding. Today honeymoon has a positive meaning but it may have referred to waning of love (honey) like the phase of a moon.

"RSVP" usually mentioned on invitations stands for French word "Respondez s'il vous plait" which literally translates to "Respond, if you please" or just "Please respond". More recent variations are "RSVP — Regrets Only" which means if unreplied, the attendance is assured.

A "bucket list" is a list of things a person wants to do before his expiry i.e. before he "kicks the bucket". The term became very popular with the release of the 2007 comedy-drama movie "The Bucket List" starring Jack Nicholson, Morgan Freeman and Rowena King.

"Air Force One" is not the name of the US President's aircraft, but it is a Radio call sign of any plane which carries the President and "Marine One" generally refers to the Helicopter in which the President travels.

"Feng Shui" (meaning "wind-water") is an ancient Chinese practice of using cosmic energy by arranging structures and landscapes to improve the lives and prosperity of people living in these spaces. However, some scientists and philosophers term it as pseudoscience.

Rainbows are caused by sunlight being reflected through water droplets acting as a prism with white light dispersing into its constituent colours. At times, when a double rainbow is seen the order of the colours in the first and second rainbow are in reverse order i.e. red and violet at opposite ends.

"Petrichor" is the smell associated with Rainfall. When a raindrop falls on the earth, air from the pores float to the surface & release 'geosmins' to which human noses are very sensitive. Camels in the desert are also very sensitive to 'petrichor' and use it to locate sources of water.

"Valentine's Day" celebrated annually on February 14th originated as Feast Day honouring early Christian martyrs named Valentines. The modern denotation symbolizing love & romance has no known record except for men & women drawing names from a jar which probably gave rise to the exchange of Valentine Card.

"Bikram Yoga" is a type of hot yoga exercise practiced in a room heated to 41 degrees Celsius with humidity at 40% intended to replicate the climate of India. The exercise consists of a fixed sequence of 26 postures devised by Bikram Choudhury, whose celebrity pupils included Martin Sheen, Susan Sarandon & Raquel Welch.

Some of the US Government's Secret Operations were oddly named as:

- Operation "Accoustic Kitty"
- Operation "Breakfast"
- Operation "Paul Bunyan"
- Operation "Chattanooga Choo-Choo"
- Operation "Paperclip"
- Operation "Toenails"

Whilst filming of the movie "Top Gun" aboard the naval carrier USS Enterprise, the director paid $ 25,000 to veer the ship to a few degrees just to capture the shot of 5 minutes of filming in the appropriate light. The film was shot during the normal operations of the US Navy.

Jimmy Carter, the former US President admitted that his son, Chip Carter smoked Marijuana on the roof of the White House with the famous musician Willie Nelson, who was performing that day at the official residence of the President.

"Fossil" fuel is a hydrocarbon occurring naturally in the Earth's crust from dead plants and animals. The main forms of fossil fuels are coal, crude oil and natural gas. Nearly 84% of the world's energy consumption and almost 64% of its electricity is derived from fossil fuels.

"Porch Pirate" is a term applied to someone who steals packages delivered to other's doorstep. With the rapid increase of e-commerce, it has become an issue of major concern.

"Chia" are edible seeds in the Mint family native to central & southern Mexico. The seeds are hygroscopic thereby absorbing upto 12 times its weight when soaked. Chia seeds are a rich source of vitamins: 'niacin' and 'thiamin' with moderate amount of 'riboflavin'. They are also rich in dietary minerals like iron, calcium, magnesium, manganese, phosphorus and zinc.

"HVAC" meaning 'Heating, Ventilation and Air-conditioning' is the use of technologies to measure and control the temperature, humidity & purity of air in an enclosed area. It can be measured by the dated "BTU" (British Thermal Unit) which is the amount of heat required to raise the temperature of one pound of liquid water by one degree Fahrenheit.

"Gymnasium" is derived from the Greek word "gymnos" meaning "naked" All physical exercises in ancient Greece were done by male members in the nude.

"Dog-Tags" are identification tags worn by military personnel. Usually worn as a pair or a single tag which can be easily broken into two. The tags contain basic information like: name, blood type, and possibly history of inoculations and religious preference. In the event of death, one half remains with the corpse, while the other half is removed for notification.

"Colours" – Black and White technically are not colours as they do not have any specific wavelengths. Human eye is capable of only seeing light with wavelengths between 380 and 750 nanometers. Beginning with violet at 380 nm it moves to blue, green, yellow, orange and ends with red at 750 nm.

"Youtube" — the inspiration to start this video streaming channel, according to co-founder Jawed Karim was when he found it difficult to locate the 'wardrobe malfunction' footage during Timberlake & Janet Jackson's show.

"Waggle" dance performed by honey bees is a figure '8' movement used as a means of communication by the bees to indicate the direction & distance to the source of nectar. The direction of the dance is in relation to the sun and the duration of the waggle signifies the distance.

A live crab is muddy-blue in colour which are formed by pigments in the shell. Upon cooking, the pigment 'crustacyanin' breaks down except for 'astaxanthin' which is a blood-red pigment hence it appears deliciously red at the dinner table.

"Mona Lisa" the portrait painting by Leonardo Da Vinci is one of the most expensive valued at around $900 million. Called "Gioconda" in Italian it was commissioned by wealthy merchant Francesco del Giocondo as a portrait of his wife. It bears a strong resemblance to the many depictions of Virgin Mary.

"British Empire" was the largest empire in history and the foremost global power. The empire held sway over nearly 25% of the Earth's total area and over 24% of the world's population. Described as 'the empire on which the sun never sets' referred to the sun shining on at least one of it's territory. Most former British colonies are members of the Commonwealth.

"Steerage" refers to the lowest class of travel on a ocean steam ship. Emigrants seeking new life in the New World were destitutes requiring cheap transportation. Passengers were allowed to travel in the ship's machinery spaces where conditions were very pathetic even resulting in several deaths.

The NATO (also ICAO) phonetic alphabet is the most widely used set of code words used in communication:

A : Alpha	H : Hotel	O : Oscar	V : Victor
B : Bravo	I : India	P : Papa	W : Whiskey
C : Charlie	J : Juliet	Q : Quebec	X : Xray
D : Delta	K : Kilo	R : Romeo	Y : Yankee
E : Echo	L : Lima	S : Sierra	Z : Zulu
F : Foxtrot	M : Mike	T : Tango	
G : Golf	N : November	U : Uniform	

"Rwandan Genocide" refers to the bloody conflict and massacre of more than half a million of the minority 'Tutsi' tribe by the majority 'Hutu' tribe in 1994. In the capital, Kigali, the genocide was led by the elite unit of the military, namely the Presidential Guards. The scale and brutality of the attacks shocked the entire world.

'Extrasensory perception' (ESP) also known as 'sixth sense' refers to envisioning things in the mind and not gained from recognized physical senses. It is a form of precognition, wherein a person perceives events of the future though skeptics discount them as a pseudoscience.

"Knot" is a unit of speed equal to one nautical mile per hour (1.852 km/h). Earlier, the speed was measured by immersing a wooden panel to the surface of the water. Knots were tied at a distance of 47 feet 3 inches passed through a sailor's fingers while another sailor used a 30 second sand-glass to calculate the speed of the ship.

"Séance" is an attempt to communicate with spirits. With participants seated around a circular table in a semi-dark room, the leader or 'medium' goes into a trance and attempts to communicate and convey messages from the spirits of the participants' dead relatives and friends.

"Mach" number is the speed of an object relative to the speed of sound. So, a plane moving at Mach 0.65 is moving at 65% the speed of sound (subsonic) and at Mach 2.0 it is moving at twice the speed of sound. It is named after Moravian born Austrian physicist Ernst Mach who even predicted the 'sonic boom'.

"McMuffin" breakfast by McDonald's was introduced by a franchisee in Santa Barbara, California, without the knowledge of the corporate office of McDonalds. Intending to reprimand the operator as McDonalds only offered lunch and dinner, it became so popular that the company embraced the breakfast concept.

United Nations Security Council was created after World War II and consists of 15 member countries of which 5 are permanent members namely USA, Russia, UK, France & China. The permanent members have the authority to veto any UN resolution. The other 10 nations are on a rotational basis based on geographic regions, each having a tenure of 2 years with 5 of them being replaced every year.

Humans in Space: As of 2022, a total of 587 humans (518 men & 69 women) from 41 countries have gone into orbit. The youngest person is Oliver Daemen aged 18 and the oldest person is William Shatner aged 90. The most space flights made by any individuals is 7 by US astronauts Jerry Ross & Franklin Chang Diaz. The longest time spent on a single mission is 438 days by cosmonaut Valery Polyakov aboard the space station 'Mir'.

The United Kingdom's Peerage consists of the following Ranks:

- Duke / Duchess
- Marquess / Marchioness
- Earl / Countess
- Viscount // Viscountess
- Baron / Baroness

"La Guardia" airport in New York came into existence when enraged Mayor Fiorello La Guardia demanded his TWA flight to be taken to New York city as his ticket mentioned 'New York' but was destined for Newark Airport as that was the only commercial airport at that time. This prompted the construction of the new airport.

The Latin name for "Lead" is known as 'plumbium' which gave rise to its symbol 'Pb' on the Periodic Table. It is attached to the end of a string to assess the vertical plane also known as 'plumb-line'. In early days lead was used to make pipes and the word 'plumber' came into being if there was a pipe-leak.

"Oktoberfest" is the world's largest beer serving festival held annually in Munich, Bavaria in Germany attracting more than 6 million visitors. It is held for 16-18 days during end of September-early October. Several cities around the world host similar celebrations modelled on the Munich event as part of the Bavarian culture.

Workers in various fields & professions are classified by the colour of 'collars' as follows:

- Blue Collar : Manual worker
- White Collar : Office worker
- Red Collar : Government worker
- Pink Collar : Service industry worker
- Gold Collar : Academic, Scientific worker
- Steel Collar : Robotic workers
- No Collar : Artists & free spirits

"Spin Doctors" is a term coined for media and public relation professionals who concoct deceptive and misleading narratives. They usually give out biased information and interpretation of a product, event or public figure in order to influence public opinion. "Spin Room" is the place where these conferences and declarations take place.

Anniversaries are celebrated as remembrances of past events. During these occasions, gifts are exchanged & some of the traditional wedding anniversary gifts are:

- 5th   : Wooden
- 10th : Tin/Aluminium
- 15th : Crystal
- 20th : China
- 25th : Silver
- 30th : Pearl
- 40th : Ruby
- 50th : Gold
- 60th : Diamond

'Cement' 'mortar' and 'concrete' are related but often get confused. Cement is a binding agent which binds other materials and hardens over time. When cement is mixed with a fine aggregate it forms mortar, a paste to hold blocks together. When cement is mixed with sand and gravel it forms into concrete, a pourable slurry material.

Myths Demystified

A common belief is that bulls get enraged with the colour red and charge at the matadors. The fact is bulls (and other cattle) are Red & Green colourblind. It is the movement of the cape that attracts the bull and not the colour.

Chameleons do not change colours to camouflage themselves from predators but do so to regulate their body temperatures or to communicate with other chameleons.

Ostriches do not bury their head in the sand. When unable to take flight or fight off their predators, they fall on the ground and pretend dead. Since they have light feathers and a thin neck, it appears as if their head is in the ground.

Sharks cannot smell a drop of blood from miles away. Though they have an enlarged brain region for detecting odours, the ocean being very huge even on a good day of currents, sharks can detect the smell of blood from a few hundred feet and not miles away.

Dogs do not pant for sweating. They pant to evaporate moisture from their tongues, nasal passages and linings of their lungs. Their 'merocrine' sweat glands are located in the pads of their paws.

Though the Sun appears yellow or orangish-red, it is in reality white and contains all the spectrums of light. The colours visible are because they have longer wavelengths than green, blue and violet. The other colours get scattered by the atmosphere.

It is said that the Great Wall of China is the only man made structure visible from space. In fact from low space not only the Great Wall but many dams, bridges, airports and highways are visible whereas further higher in space the Great Wall is only visible as a Radar image.

Common myth that a person's hair & nails continue to grow even after death is untrue. Though they 'appear' longer, its because the skin around them retracts due to dehydration of the body.

The perception that humans have 5 senses is incorrect. The senses of sight, hearing, touch, smell and taste are just the basic senses. Humans possess much more senses like 'proprioception' – which is sense of movement and 'nociception' – the sense of pain.

Brown sugar is not healthier than white sugar. The brown colour comes from a sticky residual syrup called molasses. Wash off the molasses and you will find the sugar white.

No text in the Bible states that the forbidden fruit Adam & Eve ate was an 'apple'. It could have emerged from the faulty translation of the Hebrew word 'tapuach' meaning 'scented fruit', more likely to refer to apricot or quince, as apples are not indigenous to Israel.

90% of our brain capacity remains unutilized is a common myth propagated by so called motivational gurus, hacksters, etc. Scientific data obtained from "Positron Emission Tomography" (PET) trials have proven that all parts of the brain are active even whilst performing simple tasks. Scientists have still not found any section of the brain which does not perform any function.

Not all bees produce Honey. Out of the 20,000 species of bees only 7 species of honey bees produce Honey.

Cracking knuckles does not cause arthritis. The noise emerging from the knuckles are not from the bones & joints, but it comes from the air bubbles formed in the joints.

Contrary to popular belief, dogs are not colour blind, they have two colour receptors (cones) and they can see in combinations of blue & yellow, whereas humans have 3 cones and can see in red, green & blue-violet. So instead of observing red roses, the dog may view the rose as yellowish-brown petals.

The myth that Nero played the Fiddle while Rome burned (64 AD) is untrue as the fiddle originated in the 11th century, 1,000 years after Nero. Roman historian Tacitus wrote that Nero sang during the fire, on the contrary he rushed to provide relief to the people of Rome.

Thomas Edison did not invent the Light Bulb. What Edison did was to improvise on the existing forms of lighting devices by creating the sealed vacuum bulb, improving the filament and requiring a lower voltage than the others.

All humans do not need 8 glasses of water every day. The hydration requirements are determined by the body's composition, activity levels etc. The body signals the requirement of water when needed. The level of hydration is best monitored by the yellowish colour of urine

Blood in the veins are not blue, on the contrary deoxygenated blood carried in the veins are much darker red than oxygenated blood carried in the arteries. It appears so due to the colour blue having a shorter wavelength than the colour red. As a result red gets absorbed and blue is reflected from the skin to the eyes.

Albert Einstein was not a poor student in school nor did he fail in the class 5 math subject. On the contrary he topped his class in primary school. Before the age of 15, he had mastered differential and integral calculus.

Not all of the world's deserts are hot, the polar deserts experience extreme cold like Dasht-e Lut in Iran and in Northern Greenland. Deserts are not defined by their temperatures but by the precipitation (rain) they receive.

There is not one Universal Sign Language. Just like any other language, there are several variations depending on country and region. American Sign Language (ASL) uses a one handed finger-spelling alphabet whereas British Sign Language (BSL) uses a two handed alphabet.

Eating sugar does not cause headaches. It's the rapid drop in blood sugar levels that causes headaches. Eating carbohydrate increases sugar regulating hormone 'insulin' which makes sugar levels to drop causing throbbing headache.

Urban myth that Emperor Shah chopped the hands of artisans who built Taj Mahal is untrue as no historical records exist. In fact all workers were housed in an enclave known as 'Taj Ganj' The descendants of those workers still live there and practice the skills of their forefathers.

Legal Affairs

Lady Justice derived from 'Justitia' the Roman Goddess of Law & Justice, is depicted blind-folded, carrying a sword and a set of scales (balance). The sword symbolizes the power of justice, the scales representing equality and the blind-fold representing impartiality regardless of status, wealth or power in deliverance of justice.

Perjury: The word 'perjury' derives from the Latin term 'per' meaning 'away' and 'iurare' which means 'to swear'. Perjury is the willful act of giving false testimony under oath which is considered as a contempt of court and is punishable by law.

"Libel" from the Latin "libelous" meaning 'small book', is nowadays used as a written statement to harm someone's reputation, honour or dignity, whereas "slander" means defamation by way of oral speech, or sign and gestures.

"Writ" (Latin "breve") is a formal written order issued by an official administrative or judicial body generally a Court. There are many types of writs, of which warrants and sub- poenas are the most common.

"Alibi" is a statement given by the defendant of an accused offence that he was not present at the scene of a crime and proves to be elsewhere, hence could not have committed the offence. It derives from the Latin 'alibi' meaning 'somewhere else'.

"Bail" is the conditional release of a prisoner with an undertaking to appear in a judicial court whenever required. In the USA and Philippines, bail bondsmen are individuals or firms that provide bonds for monetary gains. In most parts of the world bail bonds are considered illegal.

John Doe" (male) and "Jane Doe" (female) are fictional names used when the true identity of a person is unknown or is being intentionally concealed for legal purpose. It may also apply to an unidentified corpse.

"TASER" is an electro shock weapon designed to incapacitate people by releasing 2 barbed darts at 120 km/h. The word is acronym for "Thomas A. Swift's Electric Rifle" named after the title of a book "Tom Swift and His Electric Rifle" written by Victor Appleton.

"Mock" Trial is a legal imitation trial undertaken by students of law to rehearse the legal system in a competitive atmosphere. At times, practicing attorneys may also hold mock trials with volunteers before the real trial. Mock trials usually simulate lower court trials, whereas 'mock court" simulates appellate (higher) court trials.

'de jure' (by law) refers to practices that are recognized legally but may not exist in reality. On the contrary 'de facto' (in fact) describes practices which exist in reality but may not be defined legally.

"Grand Jury" consists of a panel of ordinary citizens representative of the community who participate in the administration of justice. Originating in England, today it is retained only in USA & Liberia. In US, it usually comprises between 16 – 23 participants.

"Blockade" is prevention by armed forces of receiving or sending out any goods or supplies and even people, from a region or country, whereas "Embargo" refers to partial or total suspension of trade rather than physical obstruction.

"Conservatorship" is a judicial court order which appoints a guardian to overlook and manage the financial and daily affairs of a minor or an incapacitated person who are unable to meet their daily needs. A conservator is responsible for establishing and monitoring the welfare and requirements of their wards.

"Polygraph" or 'lie detector test' is a procedure that records a person's blood pressure, pulse rate, respiration when exposed to a series of interrogative questions. Its accuracy is often disputed and a better alternative seems to be the 'Guilty Knowledge Test (GKT) used in Japan. In this procedure the conductor of the test has no prior knowledge of the crime nor the circumstances surrounding the crime.

"Court Martial" is conducted to try members of the armed forces of a country as per the military law. As per the Geneva Conventions a 'prisoner of war (POW) being tried for war crimes should be subjected to the same procedures as applied to its own personnel. Offences like insubordination, cowardice and desertion are purely military crimes.

'Habeas Corpus' derived from the Latin meaning 'that you have the body' is recourse in the judicial system against unlawful imprisonment or illegal detention of an individual. It is an order of the court to the custodian (e.g. prison official) to present the detainee in court to determine the legality of the detention.

Judges and advocates normally wear a black robe & a white neckwear consisting of 2 rectangular slabs denoting innocence. The two slabs represent the 'Stone Tablets' of Moses on which he inscribed the Ten Commandments. Thus the white bands represent the upholding the law of God and of men.

'Cracked Trial' refers to a trial which is to be brought up before the court on a non-guilty plea, but on that day the defendant enters a 'guilty' plea before the authorities thereby derailing the proceedings of the trial.

'Mortgage' is a loan secured to purchase real estate or to raise funds by pledging a lien on an existing property. The legal mechanism allows the lender to take possession of the property in the event of a default. The word derives from French meaning 'death pledge'.meaning that the pledge 'dies' once the loan is re-paid.

"coup d'etat" from the French meaning 'stroke of state' is a seizure and overthrow of a government and its powers. A coup is considered successful when the usurpers sieze and hold power for atleast seven days.

'Forensic science' also known as 'criminalistics' is the application of science to criminal and civil laws. Forensics is a broad field which may include fingerprint and DNA analysis, serology, toxicology, hair and fibre analysis, etc. Forensic scientists testify as expert witnesses in both criminal and civil cases and may appear either for the prosecution or for the defence in a litigation.

Sweet Cravings

Napoleon" is a French layered pastry, also called "mille-feuille" which is a French word for "thousand leaf". The word "Napoleon" is thought to have been derived from "napolitain" meaning "from Naples".

"Tres Leches Cake" is a traditional Latin American sponge (butter) cake. Its uniqueness is that it is soaked in three types of milk namely evaporated milk, condensed milk and heavy cream.

"Flan" (or "crème caramel") is a plain custard with a mold on top in which sugar syrup cooked to caramel stage is poured into the mold. It is a delicious dessert with various names & variations popular around the world.

'Knafeh' is a traditional Middle Eastern dessert made with spun pastry soaked in sugar-based syrup layered with cheese or clotted cream and topped with pistachio or other nuts and given an orange food colouring. A story mentions it being prescribed by doctors to the Caliphs during Ramadan.

"Tiramisu" ("pick-me-up") is an Italian coffee flavoured dessert made from ladyfingers, dipped in coffee, layered with a mixture of eggs, sugar, mascarpone cheese and flavoured with cocoa.

Falooda" is an Indian cold dessert made with noodles. Its origins date back to the Persian 'Faloodeh'. It is made by milk mixed with rose syrup, vermicelli, sweet basil seeds and topped with ice-cream. The word 'faluda' is at times used as a slang word to disrepute someone's reputation.

"Madeleine" is a small sponge cake from Lorraine region of France. A genoise batter is used with finely ground nuts in shell-shaped pans giving it a peculiar shell type shape. It was a beloved treat of the French Royal families.

"Affogato" ('drowned in coffee') is an Italian coffee-based dessert. It consists of a plain milk flavoured vanilla gelato or ice-cream topped or 'drowned' by shot of hot espresso. Occasionally coconut, berries and multiple flavours of ice cream are added.

"Sachertorte" is one of Austria's most famous culinary dessert created by 16-year-old Franz Sacher. During the visit of Prince Metternich in Vienna, the main chef fell ill, so his trainee created it on the spot. It is a cake with a layer of apricot jam and an icing of dark chocolate.

'Oreo' is a sweet cookie brand consisting of two pieces of biscuits with a sweet crème filling. As of 2014, it is the best selling cookie world-wide. It is distributed in more than 100 countries and over 450 billion Oreos have been produced all over the world. In due course, animal fat was replaced by hydrogenated vegetable oil due to growing health concerns.

Animal Kingdom

"Orca": The taxonomic name for the killer whale is "Orcinus orca" with "orca" being in more common use. "Orcinus" is a Latin word meaning "belonging to Orcus" which is a name for the Kingdom of the Dead.

Alligator: Alligators and crocodiles belong to distinct biological families though they resemble very similar. How to recognize them? When a crocodile's mouth is closed both the upper & lower teeth are visible, whereas only the upper teeth of an alligator are visible when their mouth is shut.

"Dodo" is an extinct species of bird (since 1662) being a direct relative of the pigeon and dove. The dodo lived exclusively on the island of Mauritius. The dodo deemed to be an awkward flightless bird and the word 'dodo' is at times used in reference to a dim-witted person.

While human eyes consist of 3 colour cones, chickens have an additional cone whereby they can also detect ultra-violet light, which is why they can sense sunrise before humans, hence their crow in the mornings. Moreover, they sense light through their pineal gland, as such even a blind chicken can sense daylight or seasonal changes.

"Emu" bird endemic to Australia is the second largest living bird after the ostrich. There was an "Emu War" in 1932 wherein the army with machine guns were deployed to divert migrating emus in which they emerged victorious. The emus were smarter and adopted guerrilla tactics by forming small formations, and the army had to be withdrawn after 50 days of unsuccessful operation.

Tail-less primates known as Apes are divided into lesser apes (Gibbons) and great apes ("Hominoids") examples of which are

- Humans
- Chimpanzees
- Orangutans
- Gorillas

"Porpoises" are aquatic mammals similar in appearance to dolphins but closely related to belugas and narwhals. They have a unique sleeping pattern, one hemisphere of their brain rests whilst asleep while the other is fully alert & thereby switching their sleep cycle alternatively.

"Myrmecology" is the study of ants, and scientists consider them as solutions to human society. They are studied for bio-diversity and conservation and lately Ant colonies are used as models in the study of machine learning, complex networks, parallel computing, etc.

Technically, all the Pandas in the world are owned by China, even cubs born in foreign zoos. Every panda is rented to zoos throughout the world on 10 year terms with rents sometimes as much as 1 million dollars per year.

Fishes have the largest number of species, more than all the birds, mammals, reptiles and amphibians put together. There are a total of 32,000 different species of fishes.

"Bull Terrier" is the only dog breed with triangular eyes and an oval shaped head. Nearly 20% of all the white bull terriers are born deaf and have a tendency to develop skin allergies. Bull terriers are considered quite stubborn in nature hence not suitable for an inexperienced owner.

"Asp" is a venomous snake found in the Nile region of Egypt. Considered as a symbol of royalty, it was used as a means of execution for criminals. Cleopatra considered it the least terrible way of dying as the venom brought sleepiness without spasms of pain. When Cleopatra herself committed suicide, she opted for the Asp bite.

Brown Bears are omnivores who consume both meat and plants. In order to execute this efficiently they have separate sets of teeth to imbibe their wide variety of diet.

Horses ("equines") are known by different names which are classified according to their sex and age as follows:

- "Foal" : up to 1 year old (either sex)
- "Yearling" : between 1 and 2 years old (either sex)
- "Colt" : below 4 years of age (Male)
- "Filly" : below 4 years of age (Female)
- "Stallion" : 4 years and older (Male, non-castrated)
- "Mare" : 4 years and older (Female)

"Zoophobia" is the general term for fear of animals. Though not all animals are feared, there is subgroup of phobias related to specific species, such as:

- "Ailurophobia" : Fear of Cats
- "Cynophobia" – Fear of Dogs
- "Ophidiophobia" – Fear of Snakes
- "Musophobia" – Fear of Mice and Rats
- "Ichthyophobia" – Fear of Fishes
- "Entomophobia": Fear of Insects

"Guide Dogs" also called 'service dogs' are trained professionally to aid, guide and protect it's master and undergoes extensive training to adapt to the owner's handicap. The dogs learn to stop at curbs, gauge owner's height relative to obstructed grounds and assist people with seizure disorders, hearing impairments and mobility issues. Labrador golden retrievers are the most common guide dogs used.

'Killer Bee' is a hybrid between the Western and African bees inter-bred by a Brazilian geneticist in 1957. Accidentally, 26 swarms escaped quarantine spreading throughout South America and arriving in North America in 1985. Apart from killing horses and other animals, they are responsible for more than 1,000 human deaths with their sting being 10 times more fatal than western honey bees.

Falcons swoop on their prey at tremendous speed with the Peregrine falcon clocked at over 200 miles per hour, the swiftest creature on this planet. As opposed to other birds of prey like hawks and eagles, falcons kill their quarry with their beaks rather than their talons.

Hybrid in biology are off-springs bred from mating individuals from two species, normally within the same genus. Some of the most common hybrids are:

- 'Liger' : Male Lion/Female Tiger
- 'Tigon' :Male Tiger/Female Lion
- 'Beefalo' : Buffalo/Cow
- 'Zebroid' : Zebra/Horse
- 'Wholphin' : Whale/Dolphin

<u>Geography</u>

The Andes Range in South America, about 4,300 miles is the longest continuous chain of mountains in the world running from Venezuela to Chile. Mt Aconcagua in Argentina is the highest peak in the Andes at 22,841 feet. The peak of Mt. Chimborazo in Ecuador is the furthest point on the Earth's surface from the center of the planet Earth.

"Pineapple Island": LANAI, which is the sixth largest of the Hawaiian Islands. The island used to be the world's largest pineapple plantation. As of 2012, the State of Hawaii owns only 2% of the island, whereas 98% is owned by Larry Ellison who is the co-founder and chairman of Oracle Corporation.

The Aral Sea covered almost 68,000 square miles in the sixties. Unfortunately, today nearly 90% is dry with less than 7,000 square miles of water left, primarily due to irrigation projects undertaken by the Soviet Union. The United Nations termed it as "one of the planet's worst environmental disasters".

"Longitude" is the distance on the east or west of an imaginary line between the North & South poles, whereas "Latitude" is a position north or south of the Equator measured in degrees. "Equator" is a imaginary line drawn around the middle of the Earth.

"Guam" is the largest of Mariana Islands and is a US territory and the first place in the US to see the sunrise, hence its motto "Where America's Day Begins". The territory was liberated from the Japanese in 1944 and nearly 13,000 Japanese were killed in the Battle of Guam.

One soldier surrendered himself in 1972 who had been in hiding for an incredible 28 years!

The Titicaca Lake lies on the border between Peru & Bolivia, is the largest lake in South America & the world's highest navigable lake. "Isa de Sol" ("Island of the Sun") in Bolivia, on Lake Titicaca is home to around 800 families and does not have any vehicles or paved roads.

Balkan Peninsula referred as "Balkans" named after the Balkan Mountains is a region in Southeast Europe. "Slavs" are the largest ethno-linguistic European group which comprises of:

- East Slavs (includes Russians, Ukrainians, etc)
- West Slavs (includes Czechs, Slovaks, etc)
- South Slavs (includes Croats, Serbs, etc)

"Macau" (also "Macao") also referred to as "Las Vegas of the East" has the richest gaming revenue in the world, 7 times more than that of Las Vegas in USA. Being the first European colony in China under the Portuguese, since 1999 it is a special administrative territory of China.

"Channel Tunnel" (also "Eurotunnel") runs between Folkestone in England to Sangatte in France. It has the world's longest undersea portion of the tunnel (23.5 miles) of it's total length of 31 miles. Trains travel at 100 miles per hour taking about 35 minutes to cross the tunnel.

"Southern" Ocean (or "Antarctic") was officially recognized as a Ocean by the National Geographic in 2021. The other official oceans are the Arctic (smallest), Indian, Atlantic and the Pacific (largest).

"Point Nemo" in the Pacific Ocean is the most remote uninhabited place on earth. The closest humans to this place are astronauts in space. It is known as the "graveyard" of all debris from space that enters the earth.

"Strait of Hormuz" is one of the world's most strategic "choke point" between the Persian Gulf and Gulf of Oman. Nearly 25% of global oil consumption and nearly one-third of the world's LNG passes through this strait making it one of the most important international trade routes in the world.

"Iraq" known as the "Cradle of Civilization" was the birthplace of several inventions like mathematics, astronomy, calendar & law code. The Sumerian people, around 5,000 BC, were practicing agriculture around the year. It was in this place, where the world's first writing system was recorded.

Costa Rica, a country in South America is bordered by Nicaragua and Panama. It has about 97% of educated population; it has been referred to as one of the 'greenest' countries and one of the 'happiest' countries in the world. It abolished its army in 1949 permanently.

"Mount Everest" at 29,035 feet is the tallest mountain in the world above sea level, but "Mauna Kea" in Hawaii is considered the tallest on the Earth. The total height from the ocean base is 32,808 feet with 13,796 feet being above sea level.

Russia, is the largest country in the world covering 6.6 million square miles is divided into 11 time zones. The time in Kamchatka is + 9 hours from Moscow time. So Russians at one end of the country would be leaving for work whilst people at the other end would be returning from work.

"Vatican City" is the world's smallest nation by area and population with an area of only 121 acres and population of around 500 people. It is a city state within the city of Rome in Italy. The head of the state is the Pope, who is also head of the Catholic Church and the Bishop of Rome. Though being inside Italy, the security of the Pope and its residents are entrusted to the 'Swiss Guards'.

"Oslo" the capital of Norway is a recycling-friendly city, it burns trash to fuel nearly half of its buildings including all its schools. Unable to generate enough trash, it imports trash from neighbouring Sweden, Ireland, England and considers imports from USA too!

"Iwo Jima" meaning 'Sulphur Island' is a volcanic island in Japan. It is here where one of the fiercest battles of World War II took place, known as the 'Battle of Iwo Jima'. All civilian inhabitants of the island were evacuated prior to the invasion of American forces and is today inhabited by only military personnel.

'Dead Sea' is a salt water lake located between Jordan and Israel. The lake's surface is 1,412 ft below sea-level making its shores the lowest land based elevation on Earth. It is one of the world's saltiest bodies of water with its salinity being 9.6 times more than the ocean. With a density of 1.24 kg/litre, swimming in this lake is akin to floating.

<u>Sports/Games</u>

Chess: The game of Chess originated in India and it evolved from a game called 'chaturanga' which translates to 'four divisions' which were:

- Infantry ("pawns")
- Cavalry ("knights")
- Elephants ("bishops")
- Chariots ("rooks")

"Bowling": The game of Bowling dates back to centuries with the pins and balls found in a tomb 5,000 years old in Egypt. Originally played with "Nine" pins, it was banned due to it being associated with gambling. To get around the ban, an additional pin was added and thus "Ten" pin bowling was born!

Tennis: To be a "Grand Slam" winner in Tennis, a player must win all the four major tournaments in the same season:

- The Australian Open (in mid-January, played on hard court
- The French Open (in May/June, played on clay)
- Wimbledon (in June/July, played on grass)
- The US Open (in August/September, played on hard court)

Lego" the famous plastic blocks, introduced in 1949 is manufactured by the Lego Group based in Denmark. The company was founded in 1934 by Ole Kirk Christiansen, a carpenter by profession. "Lego" is the Danish term "leg godt" which means to "play well". One can build among others models of celebrated structures such as:

- The Taj Mahal (5,922 pieces)
- Tower Bridge (4,295 pieces)
- The Eiffel Tower (3,428 pieces)
- The Sydney Opera House(2,989 pieces)
- The Statue of Liberty (2,882 pieces)

Martial Arts are systems and traditions of combat practiced for self-defence, physical well-being, etc. "Martial" derived from Latin 'Arts of Mars" referring to Mars, the Roman God of War. The main forms of martial arts Judo, Karate, Kung Fu, Aikido, Jujutsu, Muay Thai, etc. The "Dan" (Rank) system is applied to Japanese and some Asian martial arts and denotes the level of proficiency of the practitioner commonly recognized by the colour of the belts.

A hawk named "Rufus" was officially employed for 15 years at the Wimbledon Tennis ground to scare away pigeons. It had its own photo-card pass with the job title "Bird Scarer" and has accounts on Facebook and Twitter. It was once stolen from the trunk of his owner's car for 3 days causing "global outcry"

In Golf, holes are assigned "Par" values between 3 and 5 based on distance between teeing to putting. A 18 hole course has a par of around 72. The scorings are as follows:

- Par
- Bogey (one over par +1)
- Birdie (one under par -1)
- Eagle (two under par -2)
- Albatross (three under par -3)
- Condor (four under par – 4)

"Ping-Pong" (also "table tennis and "whiff-whaff") contrary to common belief the game did not originate in China but in Victorian England played in parlour rooms, with books being used as a net and as rackets played with a golf ball and later using cigar box lids as bats. The name "ping- pong" derived from the sounds emanating from the ball hitting the racket.

"Badminton" derived from an earlier sport called "Shuttlecock" (also "Battledore") was played by British military officers in India. The game was officially launched as a sport at Badminton House in Gloucestershire, England, and hence the name for this sport.

The standard sizes for various sports playing areas are:

Soccer: 125m x 85m with the length of penalty kick being 11.0m from the goal-post.

Tennis: 23.77m long, 8.23m wide (singles), 10.97m wide (doubles)

Cricket: Pitch length 20.12m from stump to stump with a boundary length being minimum of 64m.

Snooker: 8 feet long with a playing area being 44"x

88". Cue (stick) length being 57-59 inches.

Marathon is a road race run over a distance of 42.195 km (26 miles 385 yards) It was initially meant to be run over a distance of 25 miles, roughly the distance between Marathon and Athens in Greece. Later it was changed to 26 miles, being the distance between Windsor Castle and the Royal entrance to the White City stadium. A further 385 yards was added finishing in front of the Royal Box.

"Umpire" is an official in various sports and competition who is responsible for enforcing the rules of the game. The word is derived from old French word 'nonper' which translates into 'not even, odd number'. The alphabet 'n' was dropped as a result of being misheard. Originally an umpire was meant to be an arbiter in a dispute between two people.

"Nutmeg" is a term used in many field sports like soccer, hockey, basketball, etc. It relates to a skill in which a player kicks, dribbles, rolls or pushes a ball between the opponent's legs. It is more commonly a skill for the player to dribble and take possession of the ball behind the defender.

'Wordle' is a web-based word game founded by Welsh engineer Josh Wardle. Presented everyday a five alphabet word has to be guessed in six attempts. After every guess each letter is coloured as green, yellow or gray. Green signifies correct letter in the right place, yellow signifying correct letter but in the wrong place and gray signifies incorrect letter in the word. Following this there have been many variants and spin-offs of the original game.

Phrases/Slangs

"Drop a dime" is a slang term for the act of sharing secret information. The term apparently derived as underworld slang for someone ratting on the mob to the police. The dime was the ten-cents used to make the call.

"Paint the town red" meaning "to go on a raucous spree" relates to an event in 1837 when the Marquis of Waterford and his friends went wild one day in the town of Melton Mowbray in Leicestershire, England, wherein they actually painted the buildings with red paint.

Dough, Bread, Lettuce, Cabbage, Kale, Scratch, Cheddar, Simoleons, Clams and Moola(h) are all slang terms for "Money".

"Forty Winks" grabbing "forty winks" was suggested in a self-help book "The Art of Invigorating and Prolonging Life" by Dr. William Kitchiner in 1821. Earlier the folks took "nine winks" when getting a few moments of sleep during the daytime.

"Take a rain-check": A promise that an offer will be accepted in the future, like cancellation of an event or an item temporarily out of stock.

"Shoot the breeze": means talking idly or chatting into the wind.

"To stymie" means 'to hinder the progress' of something, it arose from the game of Golf which meant a ball blocking the path of another ball.

A "Dry Run" refers to testing of a performance or procedure before the real event. It appears to have its origin from the fire fighters in the US, wherein they would undertake practices without water, hence it being called a "dry run".

"Once in a Blue Moon" refers to something occurring very rarely. There are usually 12 full moons in a calendar year but sometimes based on solar calendars, there is an "extra" 13th full moon which is termed as a "Blue Moon", though it is not clear why it was called "blue".

"Baker's Dozen=13": In medieval England, bakers were fined or flogged if the breads did not comply with a standard size. Since it was difficult to ensure exactness of all sizes due to air content in baking, bakers would add an extra piece of bread to avoid punishment.

"To cry Wolf" means to give a "false alarm". In the fable a shepherd boy tending his sheep would shout "Wolf" to trick the villagers for assistance. Once, when actually a wolf attacked his flock, the villagers ignored his call of "Wolf", considering it as a 'false alarm'.

"To spill the beans' means to reveal information, meant to be kept secret. In Ancient Greece voters with 'yes' votes would put white beans in a jar & 'nay' votes would be represented with black or coloured beans. If someone tipped the jar, it meant revealing secrets of the vote.

Technology

"Http" stands for Hyper Text Transfer Protocol, whereas safer websites use "https" in which 's' stands for "secure socket layer".

The "www" (World Wide Web) and Internet are quite different from each other, though the terms are commonly used as the same. The Web invented by Tim Berners-Lee is a collection of documents that reside on the internet which in turn is a global network of computers. In www each document is accessible via "hyperlinks" from the vast collection of documents.

"Siri" (Speech Interpretation and Recognition Interface) is a virtual assistant that operates on Apple's IOS system. The name "Siri" is of Norwegian origin translating into "beautiful woman who leads to victory", a name the developer of the software application envisioned for his child. The female voice behind Siri in US is that of Susan Bennett. The Australian version of Siri is called "Karen" which is the voice of Karen Jacobsen and the British version is called "Daniel", the voice rendered by Jon Briggs.

"Instagram" (often 'Insta') is a hugely popular photo and video sharing app. The first photo post was that of South Beach Harbour in 2010. Two years later Facebook acquired Insta for 1 Billion dollars. At the time of sale Instagram had just 13 employees.

A QR code ("Quick Response") is a matrix two-dimensional barcode invented by the Japanese company. Denso Wave. It consists of black squares arranged in square grid on white background. The data is read by an imaging device using the Reed-Solomon error correction and is favoured over the UPC barcodes because of its greater storage capacity & fast readability.

"Fitbit" was primarily used to track & monitor the number of steps walked. Interestingly, in USA a murderer was convicted on the basis of Fitbit used as evidence. The data from the fitbit of a slain woman was able to prove that she was murdered by her husband.

SIM card is an acronym for "Subscriber Identity Module" used to identify & authenticate subscribers on telephony devices. The physical card is technically known as UICC ("Universal Integrated Circuit Card") which contains IMSI ("International Mobile Subscriber Identity") number.

"CAPTCHA" stands for 'Completely Automated Public Turing test to tell Computers and Humans Apart' is a challenge-response test in computing used to determine whether the user is a human or some automated bot.

"HP" ('Hewlett-Packard') name was decided by the toss of a coin by its founders Bill Hewlett and David Packard in which Bill won the toss. This multi-national company was started in a rented garage with an initial investment of $ 538.

"Emoji" (from the Japanese "picture" + "character") is a pictogram embedded in messages primarily to convey emotional cues otherwise missing in typed conversations. "Face with tears of joy" is considered the most popular emoji across the world, named "Emoji of the Year" in 2015.

"Skype" is an application known for VoIP, video-conferencing and instant messaging, part of Microsoft. Founded by two Scandinavians & software developed by 4 Estonians, it was originally coined as "Skyper" for ('Sky peer-to-peer') but had to eliminate the 'R' as the Skyper domain name was not available.

"Yahoo" is a web services provider, search engine, email, etc. founded by Jerry Wang and David Filo. Yahoo stands for "Yet Another Hierarchical Officious Oracle" with 'Hierarchical' meaning how its database is arranged in layers, 'Officious' meaning the office workers using Yahoo and 'Oracle' meaning 'source of truth and wisdom'.

"Spam" (or "junk") mail are unsolicited messages sent in bulk, mostly commercial in nature. It was estimated to account for nearly 90% of the total email traffic. They often contain links to phishing sites, which may contain malware as file attachments.

"Ctrl+Alt+Del" is a keyboard command on Windows compatible PC systems to terminate application task or reboot the system. Bill Gates, the founder of Microsoft once said this command was a mistake, as he preferred a single dedicated key for this function and that the "Ctrl+Alt+Del" was to be used only during the development phase.

"GPS" (Global Positioning System) uses a network of 31 satellites to deliver a location accurately from 7 meters to a pin point. The service is owned by the USA Government, spending nearly 2 billion dollars every year. So technically, the American taxpayers bear the cost for this facility enjoyed by people all over the world.

"Google" was named as a spin-off of the word "googol" which meant a very large number i.e. 10 to the power of hundred (1 followed by 100 zeroes). The original search engine was known as "BackRub" because the system checked on 'backlinks'. Founded by Larry Page & Sergey Brin, it had a third founder 'Scott Hassan' who wrote the original code of the search engine.

Surface web is generally accessed through search engines but the 'Deep' web is more than 500 times larger than the surface web. It mostly contains sites not indexed by search engines which are password protected, subscription services, login forms, etc. Further deeper is the 'Dark' web which can be accessed only through specific softwares and configurations and is mostly used for illicit and illegal transactions.

IMAX is a system of high resolution film formats with very large screens with a tall aspect ratio. In this technique a 70 mm film is run horizontally through the projector rather than vertically which results in the image being 3.4 times larger in 70 mm and about 8.3 times larger in the 35 mm format.

The computer "mouse" (called because of its shape) was invented by Douglas Engelbart at the Stanford Research Institute. Unfortunately his patent expired before the mouse became standard equipment on computers; hence he could not make any financial gains from this amazing invention!

Planetary World

Stars are classified by the colour of light that the stars emit. The classifications are ranked as O,B,A,F,G,K and M from the hottest to the coolest.

Solar eclipse occurs when the Moon passes in front of the Sun, so that the Earth falls into the shadow cast by the Moon, whereas Lunar eclipse takes place when the Earth is positioned directly between the Sun and Moon.

The days of the week are named after celestial bodies which are:

- Monday — Moon's Day
- Tuesday — Tiu's day
- Wednesday — Woden's day
- Thursday — Thor's day
- Friday — Freya's day
- Saturday — Saturn's day
- Sunday - Sun's Day

A "light-year" is the measure of distance, and not time, that light takes to travel in space, in a year which corresponds to 300,000 kilometers per second and 9.46 trillion kilometres per year. A "parsec" is the distance from the Sun to an astronomical object, which is approx. 31.0 trillion kilometres.

The following are the birth stones month-wise:

Month	Birth Stone	Month	Birth Stone
January	Garnet	July	Ruby
February	Amethyst	August	Peridot
March	Aquamarine	September	Sapphire
April	Diamond	October	Tourmaline
May	Emerald	November	Topaz
June	Alexandrite	December	Turquoise

Ann Hodges, an American woman is the only person documented to be hit by a meteorite which crashed through her roof, bounced off the radio and hit her in the thighs. A "meteor" is a piece of asteroid material that enters the Earth's atmosphere, before it enters it is known as a "meteoroid" and the chunk that survives is called a "meteorite".

A Day on the planet Venus is longer than a year. This is because the planet takes 225 days to orbit around the Sun, whereas it takes 243 earth days to spin on its own axis.

Planets take different times to orbit the Sun, which are:

- Mercury : 88 days
- Venus   : 225 days
- Earth   : 1 year
- Mars   : 2 years
- Jupiter : 12 years
- Saturn : 29 years
- Uranus : 84 years
- Neptune : 165 years
-

"Eris" planet discovered in 2005 is the reason for the planet Pluto to be relegated to the 10th place. It was declared a planet from being a dwarf planet "Eris" named after the goddess of discord is the 9th largest body to orbit the Sun

"Asteroids" are metallic or rocky bodies with no atmosphere. The majority of them are located between the orbits of Mars and Jupiter and are in various shapes and sizes. 'Ceres' is largest almost 1,000 kms across qualifying as a 'dwarf planet', while 'Dimorphos' is the smallest, about 85 metres in radius.

"Dark Matter" is a hypothetical mass which accounts for nearly 80% of the matter in the Universe. It is termed 'dark' because it is difficult to detect as it does not absorb, reflect or emit electromagnetic radiation (like light). Without this matter, some galaxies could not be formed and others would not have moved around.

"Tides". The rise & fall of sea levels is the combined effects of the gravitational forces of the Sun, Moon & rotation of the Earth. In high ('spring) tide the gravitational forces of the sun and moon act in concert thereby causing extreme movement. At low ('neap') tide the sun and moon are at right angles to each other which cancels out some of the moon's effect.

"Ursa Major" is the third largest constellation known for the asterism of its 7 stars and sometimes also called as the "Big Dipper" or "The Plough". Whereas "Ursa Minor" constellation also known as "Little Bear" is very important for marine navigation because of its brightest star "Polaris" being the North Pole star.

"Roman Calendar" was divided into 3 sections of the month based on lunar cycle. 'Kalendes' were the first days of each month (new moon), 'Ides' (full moon) fixed for the 15th of some months and 'Nones' (half-moon). The 'Ides of March' corresponds to the 15th of March, the day of Julius Caesar's assassination.

"Chinese Lunar Calendar' is based on the cycles of the Moon as opposed to the western Solar calendar. As per the Lunar calendar, a year starts somewhere between late January and early February and the year consists of 354 days instead of the Gregorian 365 days. It is divided into names of animals viz: Rat, Ox, Tiger, Hare (Rabbit), Dragon, Snake, Horse, Sheep (Goat), Monkey, Rooster, Dog and Pig.

The planets of our Solar system can be divided into 2 broad categories. 'Terrestrials' are largely composed of rocks which comprises Earth, Mars, Mercury and Venus and 'Gas Giants' which are largely composed of gaseous material includes Jupiter, Uranus, Neptune and Saturn. The planets Neptune & Uranus are called 'Ice-Giants' as they comprise less of hydrogen & helium and more elements like oxygen, carbon, nitrogen and sulphur.

The Solar System extends from the Sun and the planets starting nearest to the Sun and extending outwards are Mercury, Venus, Earth, Mars, Jupiter, Saturn, Uranus, Neptune and possible Planet 'N'.
Astronomers are still hunting for a 'Ninth' planet after mathematical evidence suggests its existence. It is believed to be 10 times the mass of Earth and 5,000 times the mass of Pluto.

<u>Food/Cuisine</u>

"Tofu" is a Japanese word meaning bean curd. Tofu is produced by coagulating soy milk using salt or something acidic. Upon the protein being coagulated it is pressed into blocks.

Miso Soup: Miso is a Japanese seasoning made by fermenting rice, barley and soyabeans with salt and a fungus to produce a paste which is then added to stock to make the soup.

"Edam" cheese derives its name from the Dutch town of Edam in northern Holland. The cheese is coated with red paraffin wax which is a layer of protection for preservation. Occasionally Edam cheese may be coated in black wax which indicates the cheese has been aged for a minimum of 17 weeks.

"Pita" is a type of bread from Middle Eastern and Mediterranean cuisines. It is usually round with a pocket in the center. This pocket is created by steam which puffs up the dough leaving a void upon cooling & meat, vegetables, pickles are stuffed into this pocket.

"Brunch" originated as a student slang in Oxford, meaning a combined meal of breakfast and lunch which is closer to the breakfast time, whereas a meal which was closer to lunch time was called "blunch".

"A La Carte" means items on a restaurant menu which are priced individually whereas "prix fixe" (or "table d'hote") is a limited choice fixed menu. Table d'hote derives from the French meaning "Table of the Host".

Olive Oil: The oil should have an acidity level of less than 2% to be called "Virgin" olive oil and Extra-virgin olive oil (EVOO) should have an acidity level of less than 0.8%

"Fra Diavolo" is a spicy tomato sauce used for pizzas & seafood, made from onions, tomatoes, red pepper, garlic, parsley/basil, olive oil. Fra Diavolo (Italian "Brother Devil") is presumably named after the revolutionary Michele Pezza.

"Moo goo gai pan" is a stir fried Cantonese dish of American version. It consists of thinly sliced chicken with mushroom in oyster sauce with vegetable additions like napa cabbage, bok choy, snow peas, bamboo shoots, etc. "Moo goo" means "button mushroom", "gai" means "chicken" and "pan" means "slices" in Cantonese.

A "Busboy" (also "Busser") is an employee in the restaurant who assists the waiting staff. Their duties include setting and clearing tables, refilling & taking dirty dishes in a wheeled cart which gave rise to the verb "to bus".

"Minestrone" is a thick Italian soup served with rice and/or pasta and lots of vegetables like tomatoes, onions, carrots, celery, leaf veggies, stock & parmesan cheese. Minestrone derives from the Italian name "minestrare" which translates "to serve".

"Chowder" soup is made from milk or cream, thickened with broken crackers, crushed biscuit, either seafood or vegetable. The name is possibly derived from the name of the utensil in which it is cooked.

"Vichyssoise" soup was invented by a French chef in America and named it after the town of Vichy in France. It is usually served cold and is a thick potato soup containing onions, leeks, and stock of cream & chicken.

Yogurt (aka "yoghurt") is made by fermentation of milk with bacterial cultures, which produces lactic acid giving yogurt its texture and acidity. It is 81% water, 9% protein, 5% fat and 5% carbs. Yogurt is a rich source of vitamin B12, riboflavin, phosphorus and selenium.

"Hollandaise" sauce is most popular in French cuisine made from egg yolk, melted butter, lime juice seasoned with salt and pepper. It is believed the French Huguenots brought the recipe to France from the Netherlands whilst returning from exile, hence the name derived from "Holland".

"Umami" a Japanese word is one of the 5 basic tastes, the others being Sweet, Sour, Bitter and Salty. It is described as "savory" having its own taste receptors first scientifically identified by Kikunae Ikeda. Foods having rich umami taste include shellfish, ripe tomatoes, cheeses, soy sauce, etc.

Coffee beans are actually not "beans" but "seeds". One method of decaffeinating the beans known as "Swiss Water Process" uses carbon filtration. Firstly, the beans are boiled in hot water and the caffeine and flavourful components are extracted. This flavour-rich water (called "green coffee extract") is then passed through carbon filter to capture the large caffeine molecules.

"Coffea Arabica" is a species of flowering plant in the family "Rubiaceae". It is believed to be the first species of coffee to be cultivated having its origins in Yemen. It represents nearly 60% of the global coffee production.

"Shakshouka" is a Maghrebi dish consisting of eggs poached in a base of tomato sauce with onions, garlic, peppers, olive oil and other spices. The dish gained international popularity after the release of a cookbook on Jerusalem cuisine by Jewish chef, Yotam Ottolenghi.

"Pumpernickel" is a heavy slightly sweet bread made from sourdough and coarsely grounded rye. Also named "devil's fart", so called because it being hard to digest.

"Saltimbocca" is an Italian dish consisting of veal wrapped with prosciutto and sage and marinated in wine, oil or salt water. The name 'saltimbocca' is the Italian word for 'jump in the mouth'.

'Chicken Tikka Masala' is a popular dish from South Asia composed of chunks of boneless chicken marinated in spices and yogurt, cooked in an earthen oven and served in a creamy sauce. As to its origin, it is understood to have been introduced in Great Britain by a migrant Bangladeshi chef.

'Molecular gastronomy'is the scientific approach to nutrition from the perspective of chemistry. It is a branch of food science that approaches the preparation of food at the scale of atoms, molecules and mixtures. It takes into account how the human senses react to mechanisms of aroma, flavor and taste.

Beverages

A "cream liqueur" is made from dairy cream like Baileys which includes Irish whiskey. On the other end "crème liqueur" does not contain cream but has lots of sugar, varieties of which include "crème-de-cassis" (blackcurrant flavour), "crème-de-cacao" (chocolate flavour) and "crème- de-menthe" (mint flavour).

"Sake" is a Japanese alcoholic beverage made from rice in a process more similar to beer-brewing wherein the rice is converted into sugars and later on fermented into alcohol. In fact, Japanese use the word "Sake" for all sorts of alcoholic beverages.

"Beer" is generally divided into Ales & Lagers, each with different brewing processes. Ales use yeasts that float on top fermenting at relatively warm temperatures for short periods, whereas in Lagers the yeasts fall to the bottom and brewed at low temperatures over a longer period of time.

"Snifter" is a short stemmed glass with a narrow top and wide bottom, used mostly to serve brandy, bourbon and whisky. The large surface area helps evaporation of the liquid, the narrow top helps trap the aroma in the glass and the narrow bottom helps the glass to be cupped in the hand.

"Soda Jerk" a pun on 'clerk' was an American term for young men who would operate the soda fountain in a drugstore. The name was inspired by the 'jerking' action, the server would make with the fountain handle back and forth when adding soda in the glass.

"Alcopop" (or 'cooler") are flavoured beverages with low alcohol volume (e.g. 3 - 7%). They may include malt beverages with fruit juices, wine coolers, mixed drinks containing distilled alcohol. Examples of alcopop are 'Bacardi Breezer', 'Smirnoff Ice' 'Hard Cola' etc.

"Champagne" is sparkling wine made using mainly 'Pinot Noir' 'Pinot Meunier' (for Red Wine) and white 'Chardonnay' grapes. Rose champagne is made from a blend of all the three grapes. The word 'Champagne' is legally reserved for wines from the Champagne region in France, under the legal structure known as the 'Madrid System'.

"Rob Roy" is a cocktail primarily consisting of Whisky and Vermouth, made by a bartender in Waldorf-Astoria Hotel in New York. It was named at the premiere of an operetta by the composer Reginald De Koven, which was loosely based upon Scottish folk hero 'Rob Roy'.

"Mimosa" cocktail is a mix of champagne (or other sparkling wine) and chilled citrus juices, usually orange served in a tall flute. It is named after the yellow- flavoured 'mimosa' plant. "Bucks Fizz" is a similar drink with twice as much of champagne than orange juice.

Milk is commonly defined by its fatty component. In order to be termed 'skimmed' milk should contain less than 0.5% fat and normally contains 0.1%. 'Low fat' is defined as milk containing 0.5 to 2% fat and milk to be labelled as 'whole' milk, the fat content must be at least 3.25%.

"Slushie" is a beverage made of slushed ice and various fruit flavours. Its invention was accidental as its inventor Omar Knedlik experienced constant issues with his

Soda fountain machine. He started storing soda in his freezer where it became slushy. When he sold this slushy to his customers, it became very popular. By 1970s, slurpee machines could be found in every American 7-Eleven store.

"Jal-Jeera" is an Indian beverage drink in which 'jal' means 'water' and 'jeera' means 'cumin' seed. The most common base is lemonade to which spices consisting of cumin, ginger, mint, black salt, pepper and some fruit powder are added. The drink aids in digestion and has cooling properties.

"Tonic" water is a carbonated soft drink originally used against malaria by addition of 'quinine'. Also known as 'Indian tonic water' it was recommended to British personnel working in the tropical climates of India to prevent malaria. Nowadays, the amount of quinine are replaced by sugary substances.

"Tea" according to Chinese legend dates back to 5,000 years when the Emperor Shennong was boiling water in the garden and few leaves from a nearby tree fell into the pot changing the colour and taste. The Emperor tried various herbs and found tea to act as an antidote.

"Linje Akvavit" an alcoholic beverage produced in Norway is distilled mainly from grains or potato, drunk during celebrations. After production the drink is sent in oak barrels from Norway to Australia and back before being bottled. Passing the Equator twice, being subjected to rocking and weather elements causes the spirit to extract more flavour and early maturation.

"Coffee" drinkers which comprise nearly 60% of the world's population should be thankful to Pope Clement VIII for this drink. When members of his court urged him to denounce it as "Satan's drink", he tasted coffee and remarked 'This drink is so delicious; it would be a pity to let the infidels have exclusive use of it'.

Root beer is a sweet soft drink traditionally made from the root bark of the sassafras tree until 1960 when the US Food & Drug Administration banned sassafras due to its carcinogenicity. Root beer is typically non-alcoholic, caffeine free, sweet and carbonated. Most root beer nowadays are flavoured with artificial sassafras flavourings.

'Cheers' and clinking of glasses as a toast has many theories as to its origin. One theory suggests that cheering loudly would ward-off any demons or evil spirits. It was also thought that the clinking of glasses would spill some drinks on the floor for the evil spirits, so that they would leave you alone.

Starbucks serves coffee in various volume sizes:

- Demi : 3 fl oz
- Short : 8 fl oz
- Tall : 12 fl oz
- Grande : 16 fl oz
- Venti : 20 fl oz
- Trenta : 30 fl oz

Wear & Tear

"Lingerie" : The word Lingerie is derived from French word "linge" meaning "washables" which is derived from the Latin "linum" meaning "linen". In French it describes any under-garment worn by either male/female. In English "lingerie" is used to describe alluring underclothing worn by women.

A "pea coat" (also "reefer jacket") is a outer woollen jacket, double breasted, broad lapelled often navy-blue coloured originally worn by European sailors. The female equivalent of the coat is known as "Jackie-O- Jacket" named after Jacqueline Kennedy Onassis.

"Tam o' Shanter" is a traditional Scottish cap, originally hand-knitted in one piece made of wool. Earlier it was made of original indigo dye (also called "blue bonnet"). The name is derived from the main character of Robert Burns's poem "Tam o' Shanter".

"Toga" is an ancient Roman garment which is a woven fabric made from white wool between 12 and 20 feet long generally worn over a tunic. It was the formal wear of male Roman citizens and the type of toga signified a citizen's rank in civil hierarchy. The female counterpart of the toga is known as a "stola".

"Parka" is a hip length hooded cold weather jacket made from warm synthetic fibre and fur-lined hood. It is the traditional clothing of the Inuit people. The parka worn by women is known as the "Amauti".

"Bermuda" shorts are the invention of tea-shop owner Nathaniel Coxon to provide his employees comfort from heat. With the shortage of clothing, Bermudan banks made shorts for their workforce modelled on the British military dress.

The "Crocodile" logo on the Lacoste brand of sportswear was named after its founder Rene Lacoste, a French tennis player who was nicknamed "The Crocodile" because of his tenacity on the court. The American press earlier named him "The Alligator".

"Bell Bottoms" (or "Flares") are style of trousers that widen knee downwards forming a Bell shape, originally used by sailors. The bell bottoms were also intended for life saving as it could be removed without removing footwear, the ends tied into a knot and inflated with air to act as a flotation device.

"Velcro" is the brand name for the hook-and-loop fasteners, commonly used in daily life. When Swiss engineer George de Mestral returned from a hunting trip he found the burs of the burdock plant stuck to his clothes. Upon microscopic examination he noticed hooks in the burs that grabbed loops in his clothing. So, he developed a product which we know today as "Velcro".

"Sari' (or "saree") is a women's garment from the Indian sub-continent which consists of an unstitched piece of woven fabric draped over the body like a robe. The length may vary from 4 to 9 metres long. Worn together with a bodice ("choli") and a petticoat ("ghagra") the sari is fastened on the waist at one end whilst the other end is loosely draped over the shoulder.

"Ascot" tie is a wide-winged neckband usually made of pale grey patterned fabric. The wide tie is normally folded and held together with a "tie-pin" and formally worn as a morning dress at weddings. The name is derived from the Royal Ascot race course. Students at the United States Army Officer School wear Ascots as part of their uniform.

"Silver Screen" synonymous with the movie industry was originally a sheet of natural or synthetic fibre used to project films. The material was coated with silver (or reflective aluminium) which provided bright pictures at all angles. The silver screen was invented by Harry Coulter Williams, a projectionist by profession.

"Ann Taylor" brand of clothes is not related to any person. The word "Ann" was chosen as it was considered to be very "New England" and the word "Taylor" signified that it was well "tailored"

"Peignoire" is a long outer garment for women made from chiffon or other translucent material. The word derives from the French word meaning "to comb the hair". So generally it refers to a sleeping gown or bathrobe when a woman combs her hair before retiring for the night.

"G-Suit" is a special piece of tight fitting pants worn by aviators & astronauts who are subject to high levels of acceleration ('g' force). This force causes blood to rush to lower parts of the body thereby reducing blood supply to the brain which may result to a 'black-out'. Inflatable bladders in the suit avoid blood pooling in the legs and abdomen by restricting drainage of blood from the brain.

"Bespoke" as applied to fine tailoring originated in Savile Row, a street in Central London. It meant a suit cut and made by hand to have an individual fit. The clients of Savile Row, the 'golden mile of tailoring' were Lord Nelson, Winston Churchill, Prince Charles, and Jinnah, the founder of Pakistan.

"Blazer" is a type of casual jacket often with naval style buttons which reflect their origins as worn by boating club members at Cambridge University. The original versions were in blazing red colour, hence the name 'blazer'. They are often part of an uniform like members of a sports team, school pupils, airline and hotel employees, etc.

'Satin' is a fabric weave having a glossy and smooth top with a dull back. The name Satin is derived from the Arabic word 'Zaytoun' which referred to the Chinese port city of Quanzhou which was a major port for shipping silk using the Maritime Silk Road to reach the Arab world and Europe.

"Sarong is a large length of fabric worn around the waist in many parts of Asia, Africa and Pacific islands. The fabric may be check patterned or bright coloured by 'bakit' or 'ikat' dyeing. Many sarongs are printed with images of animals and plants. The word 'sarong' derives from Malay origin meaning 'to cover' or 'to sheath'.

"Sericulture" is the process of silk production. Extracting raw silk starts by cultivating silkworms on mulberry leaves. In order to produce 1 kg of silk, 104 kgs of mulberry leaves must be eaten by 3000 silkworms. The top 5 silk producing nations are China, India, Uzbekistan, Brazil and Iran.

Health Facts

Ketogenic ("keto") diet is a low-carbohydrate and high- fat diet. The Liver converts fat into ketone bodies when there is not enough carbohydrates. A keto diet is sometimes prescribed to manage epileptic seizures in children.

"Vitamins" are "vital" to life in small quantities. "Vitamine" was coined in 1912 by Casimir Funk, a Polish biochemist who isolated several essential chemicals, all of which he assumed were amines. Later when determined that these vital micronutrients were not all amines, the letter 'E' was dropped from "vitamine" to give us "vitamin".

"Stevia" derived from the leaves of "stevia rebaudiana" is a sugar substitute and natural sweetener native to Brazil & Paraguay. Though the compounds in Stevia are more sweeter than sugar, the human body cannot metabolize the glycosides hence it contains "zero" calories.

Niacin is a vitamin B3, deficiency of which causes "pellagra" often described as the four D's which symbolizes diarrhea, dermatitis, dementia and death. Vitamin B is made up of 8 distinct vitamins (B1, B6, B12 etc.) Supplements like Vitamin B complex constitute a mixture of all the eight vitamin Bs.

Aerobic (also "cardio") exercises are moderate activities as contrasted to Anaerobic exercises with the difference being in the duration and intensity of the muscular contractions involved. Aerobic exercises enhance the functioning of the cardiovascular system with activities such as walking, swimming, dancing, etc.

Iris scan is at times confused with retinal scan. An iris scan is a method of biometric identification using infrared illumination as they are unique to every individual, whilst retinal scanning uses unique patterns of the retina's "blood vessels".

"pH" ('power of hydrogen') is the scale to specify the "acidity" or "basicity" of an aqueous solution. pH of 7 is considered to be neutral (pure water), solutions less than 7 are considered to be acidic and more than 7 are basic, at 25 degrees centigrade.

"Hangover" after consumption of alcohol depends upon the immune system of the consumer. It is what the bodies transform the alcohol into i.e. "acetaldehyde" a chemical sometimes 30% more toxic than alcohol.

"Snail facial": Some beauty treatments involve placement of live garden snails after thorough cleansing & moisturizing of the skin. The snail mucin contains essential nutrients difficult to find elsewhere. It has anti-aging properties boosting collagen and elastin production. It also contains 'allantoin' which is beneficial to soothe irritated skin.

The 4 main vital signs routinely monitored by medical practitioners are:

- Body Temperature
- Blood Pressure
- Pulse Rate
- Respiration Rate

"Placebo" is a inert medical substance or treatment which has no known therapeutic value. It can affect how the patients perceive changes and improvement in their condition, but have no impact on the disease itself. The 'placebo effect' is the result of the brain's role in physical health.

"OCD" (Obsessive-compulsive disorder) is a behavioral disorder, wherein an individual performs certain tasks repeatedly, thereby causing distress and impairment of general functions. Most common among them being hand washing, arranging things, re-counting etc. Noted aviator Howard Hughes as well climate activist Greta Thunberg are known to have OCD.

"Oxytocin" is a hormone produced in the hypothalamus and released by the posterior pituitary. It is released into the bloodstream in response to sexual activity and during childbirth. It plays a role in mother's milk production and bonding between the mother and newborn baby.

"Cancer" There are more than 100 types of cancers, most common among them being 'breast' 'lung' and 'colon'. "TNM" system determines the various stages of cancer wherein 'T' describes size of the tumor, 'N' describes spread of tumor to nearby nymph nodes and 'M' describes 'Metastatis' i.e. spread of cancer to other parts of the body.

Research has concluded that motorists conversing on cell phones are as impaired as drunk drivers having blood alcohol level of 0.08 % Fundamental reflex actions like braking, split second decisions such as swerving are greatly affected whilst on the phone.

"Frizzy" (or "Curly") hair are caused by 3 reasons, genetics, damage & humidity. Damage can be caused by brushing roughly or backcombing. As for humidity moisture penetrates the hair shafts causing the proteins to swell with different strands absorbing proteins in different degrees, thereby causing the hair shafts to twist and bend irregularly.

'Psychedelics' are a class of hallucinogenic drugs which causes altered state of consciousness, visual, auditory and psychological changes. The most common psychedelics in use are LSD (Lysergic Acid Diethylamide), mescaline, psilocybin and DMT (Dimethyltryptamine). Studies have shown that many are physiologically safe and rarely lead to addiction.

"Dopamine" is a chemical released by neurons to send signals to other nerve cells, thus acting as a neurotransmitter in the brain. The anticipation of rewards increases the level of dopamine. Several diseases of the nervous system are associated with dysfunctions of the dopamine system. 'Parkinsons' disease a degenerative condition is caused by loss of dopamine-secreting neurons in the brain.

'Dark Chocolate' is made from the seeds of the 'theobroma' cacao tree. In a 100 gram serving it provides 600 kilocalories of food energy which consists of 46% carbohydrates, 43% fat, 8% protein, etc. It provides various dietary minerals such as iron, copper, magnesium, manganese phosphorus, zinc and moderate amounts of vitamin B12.

'

Physiology

The Forearm is the lower part of the hand extending from the elbow joint to the palm. It is made up of the radius and ulna bones served by the radial and ulnar arteries. When the palm is held up in front, the radius bone is on the "thumb- side" and the ulna bone is on the side of the "pinky-finger".

Thyroid gland situated in the lower neck below Adam's apple, secretes "thyroglobulin" hormone for which iodine is essential. These hormones have a wide range of effects on the human body like metabolic, sexual, developmental, cardio-vascular, etc.

 "Tarsus" bone in the human body is a cluster of 7 articulating bones in each foot. They are situated between the lower end of the "tibia" and the "fibula" bones of the lower leg. In birds the tarsus have disappeared being fused with the tibia.

"Lymphocyte" is a white blood cell found in the lymphatic system that plays an important role in the immune system of vertebrates. The 3 major types of lymphocyte are "T" cells, "B" cells and "natural killer". Once they recognize invader antigens, the cells generate responses to eliminate such pathogens.

An adult human body consists of 206 bones, however at the time of birth, newborn babies have around 300 bones. In the course of development, the 94 bones fuse together to form the adult skeleton.

"Palate" is the roof of the mouth which separates the oral cavity from the nasal cavity. The anterior part is hard & bony and the posterior part is soft & fleshy. The soft palate closes the nasal passage allowing us to swallow food & drinks.

Humans shed their entire outer layer of skin every 2 to 4 weeks. Such shedding of the dead skin is known as "Desquamation". It happens when 'keratinocytes' are unnoticeably shed individually over 14 day's cycle typically.

A Nerve cell is known as a "neuron" and the long slender nerve fibre projections that transmits electrical signals from the neuron is called an "axon" and the extensions that receive signals from other neurons are known as "dendrites".

"DNA" stands for "Deoxyribonucleic Acid", a helix like structure carrying genetic instructions of all known organisms. Human DNA is almost similar (about 99.9%) yet the small difference of 0.1% is enough to determine its similarity with parents and siblings.

A Blood type ("group") is a classification of blood determined by the presence/absence of antibodies on the surface of RBCs ("red blood cells"). The main groups are "ABO" and "Rh" which determines the blood type (A, B, AB and O) with + and − denoting RhD status. Universal donors are with O Rh D negative, whereas Universal recipients are with AB Rh D positive types.

Taste buds are receptor cells also known as "gustatory" cells, that detect the 5 tastes viz: sour, bitter, salty, sweet & umami. Contrary to popular myth that specific regions detect different tastes, the fact is that any area of the tongue can detect any taste.

"Clotting" (also "Thrombosis") is formation of a blood clot inside the blood vessel preventing excessive loss of blood. When a vessel (artery or vein) is ruptured during injury, the body uses 'platelets' and 'fibrin' which is a fibrous protein to form a blood clot. Without this protective shield, an injured person would bleed to death.

"Auricle" is the visible part of the ear, also called "pinna" though this term is more oftenly used for animals. It functions differently for low & high frequencies. For low frequencies it acts as a reflector dish directing sounds towards the inner canal. For high frequencies it acts as a phase cancellation by entering the canal after a small delay.

'Myopia' or short-sightedness is an eye disorder wherein objects far away appear blurry as light falls in front rather than on the retina. On the other hand 'hypermetropia' or far-sightedness is a condition in which objects nearby appear blurry as light falls behind the retina.

'Navel' (or belly-button) is a cylindrical hollow area in the abdomen of all placental mammals which is the attachment site of the umbilical cord the conduit between the developing embryo and the placenta. The umbilical vein supplies the fetus with oxygenated nutrient rich blood from the placenta.

'Tonsils' commonly refers to palatine organs situated at either side of the back of human throat. They serve as the immune system's first line of defence against inhaled or ingested foreign pathogens. The 'M' cells in the tonsils alert the 'B' & 'T' cells that a pathogen is detected and an immune response is simulated.

"Serotonin" is a chemical neurotransmitter carrying messages between nerve cells. Nearly 90% of the serotonin is produced in the intestinal tract. It plays an important role in many physiological processes such as mood, sleep, digestion, bone health, blood clotting, etc. Insufficient serotonin may cause anxiety, depression and other health conditions.

When the muscle just below the knee is tapped, the foot involuntarily kicks forward. This reflex action takes place as a result of impulse sent along the nerves from the muscle site to the spine and back to the leg, without involvement of the brain.

Blood Plasma is a light amber coloured, liquid component of the blood bereft of the blood cells but contains all the other proteins. It constitutes 55% of the total blood volume. It protects the body from infection and other blood related disorders.

"Yawning" serves to regulate temperature of the body and brain. Yawning occurs less in colder temperatures and more in hotter environments. It is also sort of contagious in nature as one tends to yawn often when seeing someone else yawn and medical practitioners consider this reaction as a sign of empathy towards the other person who also is in need of body and brain cool-down.

"Lungs' are organs of the respiratory system in humans and most other animals. Their function is to extract and transfer oxygen from the atmosphere into the bloodstream and to release carbon dioxide from the bloodstream in a process known as gas exchange.

Religion/Spirituality

The 5 major Religions in the world followers wise are:

Religion	Founder	Holy Text	Followers (Approx.)
Christianity	Jesus Christ	Bible	2.0 Billion
Islam	Prophet Muhammad	Quran	1.8 Billion
Hinduism	Unknown	The Vedas	1.1 Billion
Buddhism	Gautama Buddha	Tripitaka	500 Million
Shintoism	Unknown	Kojiki	104 Million
Sikhism	Guru Nanak	Granth Sahib	25 Million

Buddhism has two major branches. "The 'Theravada' is the older of the two schools meaning "School of the Elders" and 'Mahayana' meaning "the Great Vehicle" split from the Theravada. "Lama" is a Tibetan word meaning "chief, high priest".

'Yuletide' celebrations coincide with Christmas. Yule was originally a Pagan festival celebrated by Germanic peoples. 'Yule' is derived from Old Norse word "jol".

A Nativity scene (also "crèche") in the Christian tradition is a display representing the birth of Jesus.

"Ring of the Fisherman" is the ceremonial Ring worn by the Pope, named after the First Pope St. Peter, a fisherman by trade. Every Pope is given a new ring with his name embossed in Latin. It was once used as a signet to seal official documents. Upon a Pope's death, the ring is destroyed signifying prevention of forged documents.

"Limbo" nowadays used to mean "in a state of uncertainty" is in fact derived from Latin meaning "ornamental border" which is located on the border of Hell. In Catholic belief, souls like unbaptized infants, who cannot enter Heaven can stay in "limbo".

The "Pieta" is a Christian art subject often depicted in sculpture, of Virgin Mother holding the dead body of Jesus in her arms. The most famous Pieta is that which is in St. Peter's Basilica in Vatican City sculpted by Michelangelo, which seems to be the only work signed by Michelangelo.

As per the Bible, Moses led the Hebrews to "Canaan" (the Promised Land) after fleeing from Egypt. Unsure of what awaited them Moses dispatched 12 envoys, each from the Twelve Tribes for assessment. Ten of the twelve, except Joshua & Caleb, falsely gave stories of Giants in Canaan, as a result of which the Hebrews wandered for 40 years in the desert. Ultimately when they finally entered the Promised Land, only Joshua & Caleb were alive, considered as God's reward.

Adam & Eve succumbed to the temptation of eating the forbidden fruit from the 'tree of the knowledge of

good & evil'. They were tempted by the serpent, as a result of which
all three were banished from the Garden of Eden, lest they eat the fruit from the 'tree of life' which would make them immortal.

"Golden Temple ('Abode of God') is spiritually the most important shrine in the religion of Sikhism, located in the city of Amritsar, India. Apart from a historical museum it houses a community run kitchen called "langar" where free meals are served to all visitors without any religious discrimination. The complex is nominated as a UNESCO World Heritage site.

"Ramadan" is the holy ninth month of the Islamic calendar observed annually by Muslims worldwide as a month of fasting and prayer. Regarded as one of the 'Five Pillars of Islam' it begins with and lasts from the sighting of the crescent moon. The pre-dawn meal is known as 'suhur' and the night feast ending the fast is called 'iftar'.

"Ten Commandments", according to the Bible, 'Moses' received the Ten Commandments which were inscribed by the finger of God on two tablets of stone kept in the Ark of the Covenant, at Mount Sinai on the peninsula of Egypt. Some of the Commandments were:

- Thou shalt not steal
- Thou shalt not kill
- Thou shalt not commit adultery
- Honour your father and mother
-

The first miracle performed by Jesus Christ was transforming water into wine. In the Gospel of John, Jesus attended a wedding feast along with his Mother and disciples

71

at Cana, when his Mother noticed the wine run out and Jesus turned the water into wine. It also signifies Christ's approval of marriage and earthly celebrations.

"Kumbh Mela" is a religious pilgrimage and festival observed in India which is the largest congregation of humans anywhere in the world. It is celebrated in a cycle of 12 years performed on the banks of 4 holy rivers. Devout Hindus take a dip in river as an act of atonement and penance for past mistakes and cleansing of their sins.

"Joan of Arc" is the Patron Saint of France honoured as a defender of France having fought in several wars against England in the Hundred Years War. At age 19, accused of heresy, which invited capital punishment, she was burnt at the stake and her charred body was again burnt twice so that the relics could not be collected.

"Rood" (or 'triumphal cross') is a life sized crucifix usually displayed on the central axis of a church. Under the rood, the Holy Cross is often displayed. At times it is also a large painting or sculpture of the crucifixion of Jesus Christ.

'Jainism' is a religion of Indian origin whose 3 main pillars are non-violence, non-absolutism and asceticism. Jain followers are strictly vegetarian and avoid root vegetables in their diet like onions, potatoes, garlic etc as a tuber's ability to sprout is considered of a higher living being. Jain monks, nuns and many followers walk bare-foot so as not to harm tiny living organisms on the ground with their footwear.

Mythology

"Osiris" In Egyptian mythology Osiris was a God of fertility, the son of "Geb" (Earth God) and "Nut" (Sky Goddess). Osiris was killed by his brother "Set", but was revived temporarily by his wife "Isis" (who was also his sister), to give birth to their son "Horus".

The "Styx River" in Greek mythology was a goddess & a river between the Earth & Underworld. According to myth, the souls of the dead had to be transported across the Styx in a ferry by "Charon". A coin would be placed in the dead person's mouth as a payment for Charon.

"Saint Elmo" (also "Erasmus of Formia") is the patron Saint of sailors, venerated when in danger of lightning and storms. The phenomenon known as "St. Elmo's Fire" is actually a plasma, caused by ionization of air molecules, when in contact with an object like the ship's mast, etc.

"Cerebus" was a multi-headed dog in Roman & Greek mythology tasked to guard the gates of the Underworld ("Hades") to prevent the Dead from leaving. The term "give a sop to Cerebus" meaning to "bribe someone off" was meant to bribe Cerebus to escape from Hades.

"Janus" was a God in Roman mythology of beginnings and endings, hence of war and peace. The month of January is presumably named after him. He is depicted as having 2 heads in the front & aft, as one looking in the past and into the future.

73

"King Tut" is a common name for the last Pharaoh of Egypt "Tutankhamun". Though his grave was robbed twice, yet it was the most nearly intact tomb found with over 5,000 artefacts. The most notable and popular symbol is the Tutankhamun Mask, on display at the Egyptian Museum.

"Achilles Heel" means weakness or vulnerable point. In order to prevent Achilles early death, his mother Thetis dipped his body in the river Styx and held him by the heel. Ironically, Achilles is said to have died by a wound to his heel, by a poisoned arrow shot by Paris.

"Santa Claus" The inspiration for Santa has been Saint Nicholas, a Greek bishop of Myra (in Turkey). He was known for his generosity towards the poor. He is the patron saint of both Moscow and Amsterdam. After his death a group of merchants removed parts of his skeleton and took them to Bari in Italy.

"Odin" is a widely revered God in Norse mythology associated with wisdom, healing, death, etc. He is frequently portrayed as a one-eyed, long bearded, spear wielding God. More than 170 names have been attributed to Odin, and has been an inspiration for artists in fine art, music and literature.

"Hera" in Greek mythology is the Goddess of marriage, women and family, Queen of the 12 Olympians and Mount Olympus and the wife of Zeus. She is portrayed as being jealous and vengeful in nature to those who offended her especially her husband's numerous adulterous affairs and illegitimate offsprings. Her Roman counterpart is known as 'Juno'.

Medical Science

The symbol "Rx" is used for a medical prescription. Regarding the origin of the symbol, one explanation is it comes from the astrological sign for Jupiter, a symbol used in olden days to invoke the blessings of Jupiter to help a patient's recovery.

"LSD" is short for lysergic acid diethylamide (known commonly as "Acid"). In 1938, Swiss chemist Albert Hofmann synthesized LSD but its psychedelic properties was discovered only when Hofmann accidentally ingested it 5 years later!

The most common Eye Chart in use (letters E FP TOZ LPED) is named after its developer, Dutch ophthalmologist, Herman Snellen and is called a "Snellen Chart".

"EEG" stands for "Electroencephalography" which records electrical activities within the neurons of the brain, whereas "ECG" stands for "Electrocardiography" which records the heart's electrical activities. EEG is instrumental in determining "brain dead" patients.

"Dialysis" of kidney, also known as 'renal replacement therapy', is the process of removal of excess water, toxins and solutes from the blood in people whose kidneys cannot perform this function. "Renal" arteries are a pair of artery that supply blood to the kidneys. Nearly 30% of the blood output from the heart are routed through the kidneys for filtration.

"Angioplasty" (or "angio") is a surgical procedure for widening of narrow or blocked arteries and veins. Also called balloon plasty, a "stent" is inserted to keep the blockage open. The word is derived from Greek "angeion" meaning "vessel" and "piasso" meaning "mould".

"Aspirin" is the trade name for the drug "acetylsalicylic acid" used to treat pain, fever and/or inflammation with a possible side-effect of upset stomach. Introduced by German company Bayer AG, it lost the use of the trade name (also "Heroin") as a result of WWI reparations paid by Germany and hence became a generic product.

"MRI" (Magnetic Resonance Imaging) is a medical scanner which uses magnetic fields and radio waves to generate images of the anatomy. However, some patients may feel uncomfortable with this procedure, due to the longer and louder durations spent inside a confined chamber. Also it may exclude some patients having metal implants inside their body.

"Colonoscopy" is the internal imaging of the large intestine and part of the small intestine by a fibre optic camera mounted on a flexible tube passed through the anus. Such examinations can detect gastrointestinal haemorrhage, polyps and colon cancer, but commonly done to diagnose inflammatory bowel disease.

"ACE" (Angiotensin-converting-enzyme) inhibitors are medications used for treatment of blood pressure and cardiac related issues. It causes relaxation of blood vessels which lowers the blood volume and decreases the demand for oxygen from the heart. The first inhibitor was developed from the venom of the deadly pit viper snake in Brazil.

'Pharmacopoeia' is a publication containing description and directions for the use of medicinal compounds issued by a Government authority or pharmaceutical society. The directions for preparation of medicines are known as 'monographs'. The initial major work in this field is the 'Pliny's Pharmacopoeia'.

'Nissen fundoplication' is a laparoscopic surgery performed to treat 'gastroesophageal reflex disease' (GERD). In this procedure the upper part of the stomach is wrapped and stitched around the lower end of the esophagus. GERD also known as 'acid reflex' is a condition in which stomach acid flows up into the esophagus causing heart-burn, etc.

'Perfusionist' is a member of the cardiac surgery team who operates the cardiopulmonary bypass (heart-lung) machine by maintaining blood flow to the tissues. A perfusionist is responsible to monitor & maintain the patient's oxygen and carbon dioxide levels, blood circulation, drug levels, etc.

'Ultrasound' or 'Sonography' is a medical imaging procedure to probe body's internal organs, muscles, blood vessels etc. It is composed of sound waves with frequencies higher than humans hearing range (>20,000 Hz). The pulses from the probe echo off the tissues with different reflection properties.

'Tracheostomy' is a surgical procedure performed on patients with acute breathing problems. An incision (cut) is made on the anterior (front) of the neck thereby opening a direct airway path to the trachea (windpipe), allowing the patient to breathe without the use of nose or mouth. It may also be recommended for people with 'obstructive sleep apnea'.

'Auscultation' is the listening of sounds of bodily organs through a stethoscope. Doctors study three main organs, the heart, lungs and gastrointestinal system. Abnormality in breathing patterns, heart beats etc. enables health professionals to recommend more advanced diagnosis of the patient.

'Electromyography' (EMG) is a diagnostic technique to evaluate and record the electrical activity of the skeletal muscles. It detects the electric potential generated by the muscle cells. These signals can be analyzed to detect abnormalities, activation levels and biomechanics of human movement.

'Caesarian' or C-section is a surgical procedure performed in the delivery of baby or babies through an incision in the mother's abdomen. Reasons for such a procedure may be necessitated due to obstructed labor, twin pregnancy, high blood pressure of the mother or complications with the placenta or umbilical cord.

"Positron Emission Tomography" (PET) is an imaging technique used in the diagnosis of certain bio-chemical processes of the organs e.g. glucose metabolism and oxygen uptake. In this procedure a chemical compound of carbon, oxygen, nitrogen, fluorine is injected into the body. The data from the detectors are analyzed, integrated and re-constructed to produce images of the organs being scanned.

Corporate Affairs

The fashion goods company Prada was established by two brothers Mario & Martino Prada in 1913 in Milan. Mario was against women of the family joining the family business. Interestingly & ironically upon his demise, his son was uninterested in the family business so his daughter took over & ran the company & later handed it over to her daughter.

ASICS is a Japanese corporation from Kobe which produces sportswear, founded by Kihachiro Onitsuka in 1949. The name is an acronym of the Latin phrase "anima sana in corpore sano", which translates to "a healthy soul in a healthy body". Nike Inc. (previously known as Blue Ribbon Sports) was founded as a Sales Agent for the Onitsuka Tiger Shoes in the US.

The RCA (Radio Corporation of America) logo features a dog named Nipper. Nipper was a real dog from England whose owner, Francis Barraud, made a painting of Nipper listening to a gramophone and he himself came up with the tagline "His Master's Voice".

Frito-Lay now is a wholly owned subsidiary of PepsiCo, manufacturing potato snacks like Fritos, Cheetos, Doritos, etc. Frito Corp was started by Elmer Doolin in 1932 in his mother's kitchen and started selling the chips from the trunk of his car. Whereas Lay chips was started by Herman Lay in 1938, being hand-made until he invented the first potato processor in 1948, whereupon potato chips spread all over the world.

Diageo plc. is a London based multinational beverage company operating in more than 180 countries and having production facilities in more than 140 sites around the world. It owns some of the world's famous alcoholic brands, viz:

- Whisky: Johnnie Walker, Black & White, Seagram's, Crown Royal, Talisker
- Beer: Guinness
- Vodka: Smirnoff, Ketel One
- Rum: Captain Morgan
- Liqueur: Baileys
- Gin: Gordon's, Tanqueray
- Tequila: Don Julio

"Adidas" was founded by Adolf "Adi" Dassler along with his brother Rudolf in Bavaria, Germany in his mother's laundry room. Known earlier as Dassler Shoes, the two brothers split up with Adi-Dassler forming "Adidas" and Ru-dolf Da-ssler forming "Ruda" shoes which was later re-branded as "Puma". Adidas's big break came when Adi persuaded American Jesse Owens to wear his shoes at the 1936 Berlin Olympics, wherein he won 4 Gold medals.

The famous "Barbie" doll is the creation of American businesswoman Ruth Handler, the wife of Mattel Toys co- founder. Barbie was inspired by German toy doll "Bild Lilli". "Barbie" and her male friend "Ken" have been the two most popular toy figures in the world.

Apple Inc. largest acquisition so far has been that of Beats Electronics for a whopping 3.4 billion dollars. Beats was co-founded by American rapper Dr. Dre, and the company is primarily into manufacturing Audio products such as speakers, headphones, ear buds & car audios.

"Gucci" is a high-end Italian fashion house founded by Guccio Gucci and is currently a subsidiary of French luxury group "Kering". Gucci became a world-wide brand under the management of his son Aldo Gucci. However, due to family feud Aldo's son Paolo got him jailed for one year at the age of 81, for tax evasion of 7 million dollars.

The world's oldest operational company is Kongo Gumi, a Japanese construction company, which is more than 1,400 years old, founded in 578 CE. In 2006, the company going through hard times went into liquidation, being purchased by the Takamatsu Group.

Coca-Cola was invented by John Pemberton as a patent medicine to wane away from his addiction to morphine. The formula of the recipe has been the most guarded trade secret and was also used as a collateral to obtain a bank loan. The original copy of the formula has been held in the Truist Financial's main vault in Atlanta, USA for 86 years.

Omega SA is a Swiss based luxury watch maker since 1848. The "Omega Speed master" was the first watch on the Moon worn by Buzz Aldrin, it has been the Official Time- keeper of the Olympic Games since 1932 and James Bond 007 has been wearing an Omega watch in films since 1995.

"YSL" (Yves Saint Laurent) was a French fashion designer, worked as an assistant to Christian Dior. He suffered mental break-down as a result of hazing by fellow soldiers in the army, was on psychoactive drugs and electroshock therapy.

After his release from hospital he started his own fashion brand YSL and among others designed the wedding dress of Shah of Iran's wife.

"OXO" brand of kitchen appliances and housewares were designed for physically challenged people. The idea for such tools arose when the founder Sam Farber, noticed his wife having difficulty in gripping ordinary appliances due to mild arthritis. The brand was ultimately acquired for $273 million by Helen of Troy Ltd.

"Wal-Mart" is a multinational corporation operating stores and hypermarkets worldwide. It is the world's largest company by revenue ($ 570 billion) annually and the largest private employer in the world (2.2 million employees). Founded by Sam Walton, his heirs own more than 50% of the company's equity.

SAAB is a defunct automobile manufacturer from Sweden that was partially and then fully owned by General Motors (GM). In 2010, Saab was sold to Dutch manufacturer Spyker Cars N.V. In 2011, SAAB applied for bankruptcy when GM opposed its sale to a Chinese consortium on the grounds of transfer of technology. NEVS lost its licence to manufacture cars under the SAAB name, hence marketed under the new designation 'NEVS'.

Estee Lauder is a multi-national cosmetics company second largest in the world after L'Oreal. Lauder launched her first fragrance 'Youth Dew' a bath oil. It became so popular that instead of using a few drops behind the ears, women emptied entire bottles in the bath tub, thereby raising her sales from 50,000 bottles to 150 million!

Celebrities

Supermodel "Iman" was born as Zara Mohamed Abdulmajid in Somalia & renamed Iman which is Arabic for "faith". She was married to rock star David Bowie until his death in 2016. She is also an entrepreneur, owning Iman Cosmetics with her signature fragrance "Love Memoir" and owns apparel firm Global Chic. She is a linguist, fluent in Arabic, Amharic, Italian, French & English.

The main antagonist in the James Bond movie "Goldfinger" was played by German actor Gert Frobe who was a member of the Nazi Party, as a result of which the movie was banned in Israel. But when two Jews claimed that Frobe gave them shelter and helped them escape from the Nazi authorities, the movie was exhibited in Israel.

Nora Ephron was a successful author, script-writer and director of acclaimed movies like "You've Got Mail" and "Julie & Julia". She was one of the few people who knew the identity of "Deep Throat" the informer of Watergate scandal co-authored, by her husband Carl Bernstein. In her autobiography, she revealed about her husband's illicit affair with Margaret Jay, the daughter of British Prime Minister, James Callaghan.

"Les Paul" was a legendary American Guitarist and inventor of the "Gibson Les Paul" guitar. During a car crash he shattered his right arm and elbow. Refusing to be amputated, he suggested the surgeons to rebuild and position his arm just under 90 degrees such that he could hold & play the guitar.

Ella Fitzgerald also known as "First Lady of Song" and "Queen of Jazz" was an American singer who went through a tumultuous adolescence. Losing her mother at age 15, ill-treated by her stepfather, she worked as a lookout for a brothel and as a numbers runner for the Mafia. In Amateur Nights, at the Apollo theatre she got a break to sing and a Star was born!

Jennifer Hudson is an American actress & singer who was a finalist on "American Idol" in 2004. She is the youngest woman & second coloured woman to win the Grand Slam of movies "EGOT" (Emmy, Grammy, Oscar, Tony awards). In 2008, her mother, sister and nephew were shot dead by her brother-in-law.

"Bono" the lead vocalist of rock band U2, is known for his activism, and philanthropy for humanitarian causes. However, once having forgotten his hat in London whilst on a concert tour to Italy, he had his hat flown on a First Class ticket.

"27 Club" is a notional club listing the names of popular musicians, artists and celebrities who 'died' at the age of
27. Among the others were these famous personalities:

- Amy Winehouse
- Jimi Hendrix
- Janis Joplin
- Brian Jones
- Jim Morrison
-

Oprah Winfrey dubbed as "Queen of all Media" is a TV show host, producer, actress, and author. She was once the world's only black billionaire and the richest African-American of the 20th century. But she had a traumatic childhood, born into poverty she would wear dresses made from potato sacks. Molested at the age of 9, she gave birth to a premature child at age 14 who died after birth. However, destiny had grand plans in store for her!

Kathryn Bigelow is the first woman to win the Oscar Award as a Director of the film "Hurt Locker". Married to James Cameroon of 'Titanic' fame, she was on Time 100 list of most influential people of the year in 2010. Her other successful movies included "Zero Dark Thirty" and "Point Break".

"Selena Gomez" is a young artiste who is the most followed musician and actress on Instagram with over 344 million followers. Raised in abject poverty, she rose to become one of the most sought after celebrity by leading brands. She has dated Nick Jonas & Justin Bieber. At this young age, she has several health issues like lupus, bipolar disorder and even underwent a kidney transplant.

"Lady Gaga" (nee 'Stefani Germanotta') is reportedly paranoid about ghosts specifically one named 'Ryan'. She has installed Electro Magnetic Field meters worth $50,000 to detect on poltergeists. Before her performances anywhere in the world, a team of paranormal investigators precede her visit to scan the venue.

"Paris Hilton" is a billionaire heiress of the Hilton chain of Hotels. All of her pet dogs have their own Insta account which would be the envy of most influencers. They have their own Spanish styled villa in Los Angeles, with designer furniture and fittings measuring 300 sq. feet costing a whopping $325 000/-

J.K. Rowling, the author of 'Harry Potter' is one of the most successful writers having sold more than 500 million copies world-wide, translated into more than 70 languages. Developing the concept of the story on a delayed train from Manchester to London, her book was initially rejected by all the major publishers. Being divorced and penniless, she suffered bouts of depression and even enrolled for government welfare support.

Arnold Schwarzenegger, regarded as one of the greatest body builders, won the Mr. Universe title at age 20. Born with a defective aortic valve, he played various sports before becoming a body-builder. Initially, unaccepted in Hollywood due to his Austrian accent he was offered B-Grade films. Ultimately, he went on to become the Governor of California, USA.

"Angelina Jolie" admitted to having mental issues and suicidal thoughts early in life. Unwilling to take her own life, she tried to hire someone to have her murdered. The person dissuaded her and asked her to contact him after 2 months during which time she changed her mind to die

<u>Personalities</u>

"Buzz" Aldrin was the second person to set foot on the Moon along with Neil Armstrong. A science graduate from MIT, he was a jet fighter pilot, flew 66 combat missions during the Korean War and shot down 2 MIGs. Honoured by numerous Bravery Medals, after leaving NASA, he struggled with clinical depression and alcoholism, also being arrested for disorderly conduct, as revealed in his autobiography "Magnificent Desolation".

Albert Einstein's brain had a interesting journey after his death. The pathologist who conducted his autopsy Dr.Thomas Harvey kept his brain to study any abnormality for his brilliance. Parts of his brain were given to various scientists to study but no conclusive evidence was found to be different than an average brain though one study claimed of an extra groove on his frontal lobe.

Some of Shakespeare's most notable words were:

- All that glitters is not gold!
- Uneasy lies the head that wears the crown!
- Rose by any other name, would smell as sweet!
- All the World's a Stage!
- The robbed that smiles, steals something from the thief!
- To be or not to be: that is the question!
- Neither a borrower nor a lender be!
- A man can die but once!

Laila Ali, daughter of boxing legend Muhammad Ali, herself a professional boxer, never lost or drew a fight in her career. She has a record of 21 knockouts in her 24 wins including that with Jackie Frazier-Lyde, daughter of Joe

Frazier the arch rival of Muhammad Ali. Before her boxing career Laila was a manicurist with her o w n nail salon.

Oskar Schindler was a German industrialist who saved the lives of 1,200 Jews during the Holocaust in WWII. He is the subject of the book "Schindler's Ark" and its film adaptation "Schindler's List". After his bankruptcy, he was supported by Jewish groups of the people he saved. He is the only member of Nazi Party to be buried on 'Mount Zion'.

'Patty Hearst' 19 year old granddaughter of billionaire media magnate was kidnapped by a guerrilla outfit SLA. She later joined the same group and assumed the name 'Tania' and even participated in a bank hold-up robbery along with the gang in San Francisco. She was sentenced to 35 years imprisonment later reduced to 7 years.

"Naomi Osaka" is the First Asian player to be ranked No.1 in the Women's Tennis Association and is a four times Grand Slam Singles champion. In 2020, she was the highest earning female athlete of all time. She was also the first tennis player to light the Olympic cauldron during the Opening Ceremony.

Henri Dunant was Swiss a businessman and founder of the Red Cross Society which provides humanitarian aid all over the globe. He was the first recipient of the Nobel Peace Prize. Whilst on a business trip to Italy, he witnessed the suffering of soldiers in the Battle of Solferino, which led him on the path of selfless service.

"Dian Fossey" was an American primatologist who studied Gorillas in the wild. She spent 20 years in the jungles of Rwanda a n d her scientific studies were published in a book which was adapted into a 1988 film 'Gorillas in the Mist'. Unfortunately, she was brutally murdered in her cabin in the forest, presumably by poachers.

"Jill Biden" is the First Lady of USA since 2021 and been the 2nd Lady of USA from 2009 to 2017. Being an educator and Professor of English, she has been the first wife of a President or Vice-President to hold a regular paying job whilst her husband held Office. She has authored the book 'Where the Light enters: Building a family, Discovering Myself'.

Usain Bolt (aka "Lightning Bolt") is a Jamaican sprinter and the most successful male athlete. He is the world record holder of the 100 metres, 200 metres and 4x100 metres relay. He is the world's only sprinter to win 100 metres and 200 metres in a row at the Olympic Games. He holds the world's fastest records of 9.58 seconds in 100 metres and 19.19 seconds in 200 metres.

"James Bond" is a fictional spy character created by writer Ian Fleming. The name was taken from a real person who was a Caribbean bird expert and the code "007" (double O- seven) was taken from English secret agent John Dee who would sign his reports as a stylized "007" to Queen Elizabeth I, meaning for "Her eyes only".

J. Paul Getty, was an American petroleum industrialist and one of the richest man in the world, but very frugal by nature. When his grandson was kidnapped in Rome and his ear sent by post, he negotiated with the kidnappers and brought down their original demand of $ 17 million to $ 2.2 million. The grandson, Getty III, was severely traumatized and became a drug addict. As a result of overdose, he was rendered speechless, nearly blind & paralyzed until his death.

"Curie" family have been the most awarded Nobel laureates till date. Irene Curie along with her husband Frederic were awarded the Nobel in Chemistry as were her parents Pierre and Marie Curie. Unfortunately, both mother and daughter died of illnesses as a result of high exposure to radiation. The papers of Marie, including her cook-books are stored in lead-lined boxes, as it is considered too dangerous to handle.

Colonel Sanders" held number of low paying jobs during his career from labourer to practicing law, but was left penniless. Contemplating suicide at age 65, he decided to give life a last shot and started selling fried chicken to filling stations and restaurants along the highway on commission basis. Had he ended his life, the world would not have been able to taste Kentucky Fried Chicken (KFC)

'Mother Teresa' (born Anjeze Gonxhe Bojaxhiu) was an Albanian born nun who dedicated her life to selfless services to the downtrodden poor of India. She was the founder of Missionaries of Charity operating in more than 133 countries. She was the recipient of Nobel Peace Prize and was canonized as 'Saint Teresa of Calcutta'.

Igor Sikorsky was a Russian-American pioneer in aviation in both the fixed-wing aircraft and helicopters. He was the developer of the first ocean-crossing flying boats for Pan American Airways, in their Clipper era.. His designed Sikorsky-R-4 helicopter became the world's first mass-produced helicopter in 1942.

Flora & Fauna

Fauna, Flora, Funga and other forms of life are collectively known as "biota". Fauna is described as the animal life of a particular area or region, named after "Fauna" the Roman Goddess of Earth and Fertility, and Flora is the plant life of a particular area or region, named after "Flora" the Roman Goddess of flowering plants.

The largest seed of a plant on earth is that of the "coco de mer" palm tree, whereas the coconut is the second largest. Palms are perennial flowering plants with many forms like vines and shrubs. Some are shaped like a tree with a woody stem & leaves which we know as "palm trees".

Papyrus" (or "Nile Grass") is a aquatic flowering plant native to the Nile Delta of Africa. It is the source of papyrus paper one of the first type of paper used notably by Ancient Egyptians. Earlier to that the most common surface for writing was parchment, made from animal skins.

Herbs & Spices are consumed for macronutrients and are used for flavouring food with aromatic and savoury properties. Herbs generally refers to the leafy green or flowering parts of a plant, whereas Spices are produced from other parts of the plant like, seeds, bark, roots, and fruits.

Teak Wood is a hardwood tree native to Southeast Asia, mainly Myanmar & Thailand. It is the preferred medium for outdoor furniture and construction due to its weather resistant properties as well as its natural oils being termite and pest resistant.

91

"Sap" in a plant consists of two types, the "xylem" and "phloem". The xylem is the watery solution of minerals and other nutrients which moves from roots towards the leaves. The phloem sap consists primarily of sugars, it moves from where sugars are produced to the parts of the plant where sugar is used.

"Cranberries" are low creeping vines, which are initially green but turns red when ripe. They have 4 air pockets which allows them to float and also to bounce. Farmers use this feature to determine the ripeness of the berry. The bounce means they are nice and firm.

"Wisteria" is a genus of flowering plants in the legume family. They climb by twining their stems around any available support. The Japanese wisteria twines clockwise whilst the Chinese wisteria twines counter- clockwise. The world's largest known wisteria is more than 1 acre in area weighing 250 tons.

"Rainforests" and "Jungle" are different. 'Rainforests' are characterized by a closed and continuous canopy of trees with the ground below clear of vegetation due to lack of sunlight. 'Jungle' is land covered by dense forest and vegetation. Tropical rainforests are called "World's largest Pharmacy" as over 25% of natural medicines were discovered in the rainforests.

"Cardamom" are seeds of plants native to the Indian sub-continent, used as flavouring and spices in food, drink & medicine. The plants were introduced in Guatemala by German planter Kloff and today Guatemala is the largest producer & exporter in the world. It is the third costliest spice in the world by weight, after saffron and vanilla.

"Guar gum" is extracted from guar beans, it is an off- white powder used in the food and feed industries, mainly in gluten-free products. India produces nearly 65% of the world's guar gum.

"Calabash" ('bottle gourd') is a vine grown for its fruit. It can be consumed as a vegetable or used as a utensil, container or musical instrument. It is the world's first plant cultivated not only to be consumed as a food but also to be used as a container for storage, smoking pipe and as an equipment for enema.

"Arboriculture" is the study of individual trees, shrubs, vines, which looks after the health and cultivation of stand-alone trees and plants rather than forestry which looks after the welfare of the entire forest biome.

"Bamboo" plant is the fastest growing 'grass' in the world, with a growth of nearly 36 inches in 24 hours. Bamboo shoots are used in many Asian cuisines and it is comprises nearly 99% of a Panda's diet. Other uses of bamboo consist of fabrics, musical instruments, furniture, construction, etc.

"Oleander" is a beautiful flowering shrub used as an ornamental and landscaping plant. It is considered a poisonous plant because it contains compounds like 'oleandrin' which is toxic especially to animals when ingested in large amounts. In humans, it can affect the gastrointestinal, cardio-vascular and central nervous systems.

Bananas undergo a colourful transformation from deep green to brownish black. Most fruits produce a hormone 'ethylene' which enables the maturing and ripening process. Unlike most fruits, bananas produce larger amounts of ethylene causing it to over ripen rapidly causing the yellow pigment to form brown spots in a process called 'enzymatic browning'

What makes 'saffron' the most expensive spice in the world? Saffron is actually a purple flower and the yellow sweet smelling part of the flower is the stigma which are just 3 nos in each flower. As such it takes almost 75,000 flowers to make just 1 pound of this spice. Furthermore, the harvesting process is not mechanized and has to be manually picked by hand.

Raw tomatoes are rich in 'chlorophyll', a phytochemical which gives it the colour green. As it ripens it undergoes changes as chlorophyll breaks down and 'lycopene' is produced which changes it's colour into red and in softness.

'Vanilla' is a spice obtained from the pods of Mexican species for which pollination is required to produce the orchid from which vanilla is extracted. It was 12 year old enslaved child Edmond Albius who discovered that it could be hand pollinated which allowed global cultivation. It is the world's 2nd expensive spice after saffron.

"Lavender" is a genus of flowering plants in the mint family. There is a 'colour' named after the shade of its flower. It has been used since centuries in traditional medicine and cosmetics. It is also used as ornamental plants, culinary herbs and essential oils.

Money Matters

VISA Inc. is a multi-national financial services company, head-quartered in California, USA. Visa does not issue any credit or debit cards, instead it sets up payment gateways and electronic infrastructure to banks who then display the Visa logo on their transaction cards. It facilitates electronic fund transfers throughout the world.

The most expensive object ever made is the ISS (International Space Station) costing nearly 150 Billion dollars and billions every year for its maintenance. The living quarters on the ISS is roughly equivalent to a 6-bedroom house including a gymnasium.

'Fort Knox' is a facility known as United States Bullion Depository. Most of the US Gold reserves are in Fort Knox, but the biggest gold depository is in the vaults of the Federal Reserve Bank of New York in Manhattan, which mostly belongs to foreign banks and nations.

"GNP" (Gross National Product) & "GDP" (Gross Domestic Product") are different. GNP is the total income of the residents of a country world-wide, whereas GDP refers to the total income of the residents within geographical boundary of the country.

In stock exchange parlance, a "Bull" market is termed when there is optimism among the traders and a "Bear" market is when there is despondency about the shares. The terms emerged from how the animals attack with the "bull" bucking upwards with its horns and the "bear" clawing downwards with his paws.

The "Credito Emiliano" Bank in Italy accepts Cheese as collateral against loans to dairy farmers. The banks temperature controlled vaults can store 440,000 giant wheels of Parmigiano-Reggiano cheese until they are matured and ready for sale.

"Arbitrage" is the practice of trading in stock shares by taking advantage of a difference in prices in two or more markets, thereby earning a profit from the difference. Persons engaged in arbitrage are known as "arbitrageurs".

"Angel Investor" is an individual who provides capital to a business start-up, usually in exchange for equity ownership. The word "angel" has its roots in Broadway theatre, wherein wealthy individuals would finance theatrical productions, which could otherwise shut- down. Nowadays, in arts the word "patron" is more commonly used instead of "angel".

"Euro" Coins are issued by the 19 European countries. The 'reverse' side of the coins contain a common design used by all the countries, whilst the 'obverse' side contains the design of each specific nation. The French coin depicts an 'oak & olive branch', Irish euro features an 'harp', the 'Maltese cross' is on the currency of Malta and the Belgium coins depict the 'Kings of Belgium'.

"IPO" (Initial Public Offering) is the sale of a company's shares to individuals and institutional investors. It enables the company to raise funds for their functioning and expansion. Details of the proposed offering are disclosed in a document called 'prospectus'. It is normally underwritten by one or more Investment banks who arrange for the listing of shares on one or more Stock Exchanges.

"Unicorn" in business terminology, is a private start-up company with a valuation of over $ 1.0 billion known as an Unicorn, a reference to the mythical creature considering the rarity of such ventures. Companies with over $ 10 billion valuations are known as "Decacorns". Some of the prominent decacorns are SpaceX, Stripe, Bytedance, Instacart and Klarna.

International Exchange Rates can be fixed (pegged), floating or a hybrid of both. It is regarded as the value of one country's currency in relation to another currency. A floating rate exchange is affected by the economic actions of the country's Central bank.

Life span of US Dollar Bills are approx. as follows:

- $ 1   : 18 months
- $ 5   : 2 years
- $ 20   : 4 years
- $ 100 : 9 years
- Coins: 30 years

Whilst most paper currencies in the world are made from wood pulp, interestingly the US currency is made from a blend of 75% cotton and 25% linen.

The 1913 Liberty Head Nickel is an American 5 cent piece minted in limited quantity unauthorized by the US Mint. It is one of the most highly prized and coveted rarities in the history of American numismatics. One of these pieces was sold for 5 million dollars.

"Dirty Money" is usually referred to money obtained unlawfully, but the literal translation also holds true, as it is found that 94% of the bills are contaminated with bacteria, while nearly 7% are infected with deadly pathogens.

The 'Great Depression' of 1929 began as a result of fall in United States stock prices on October 29th known as 'Black Tuesday'. It was the longest and most widespread depression of the 20th century affecting countries around the world. The GDP (Gross Domestic Product) of countries worldwide fell more than 15% and unemployment rose to as high as 33%.

'International Monetary Fund' is a financial institution of the United Nations having more than 190 country members. Countries contribute to a pool through a quota system under which countries experiencing balance of payments problems can borrow from the Fund. IMF is regarded as the global lender of last resort. It is mandated to monitor the economic and financial policies of its member countries.

Pablo Escobar, the notorious drug cartel boss is estimated to earn $50 million in cash every day and spending nearly $2,500 in rubber-bands to hold the cash together He is reported to have lost nearly $2.1 billion cash to rats and other elements eating away his cash in the warehouses and burning $2 million in cash to keep his daughter warm during a winter season.

Conclusion

Hope this compilation has added value to the readers experience.

Since the world of knowledge is so immense, not all subjects could be compiled in this edition, like Arts, Literature, Entertainment, Sciences etc; which shall be included in later editions.

So, keep the fire of curiosity alive and never stop learning!

www.ingramcontent.com/pod-product-compliance
Lightning Source LLC
Chambersburg PA
CBHW071924120726
48001CB00005B/1866